Cosmic
Whispers

Cosmic Whispers

Niyi Afolabi

AFRICA WORLD PRESS
TRENTON | LONDON | CAPE TOWN | NAIROBI | ADDIS ABABA | ASMARA | IBADAN | NEW DELHI

AFRICA WORLD PRESS
541 West Ingham Avenue | Suite B
Trenton, New Jersey 08638

Copyright © 2019 Niyi Afolabi

All rights reserved. No part of this publication may be reproduced, stored in a retrieval system or transmitted in any form or by any means electronic, mechanical, photocopying, recording or otherwise without the prior written permission of the publisher.

Book design: Dawid Kahts
Cover design: Ashraful Haque

Library of Congress Cataloging-in-Publication Data

Names: Afolabi, Niyi, author.
Title: Cosmic whispers / Niyi Afolabi.
Description: Trenton : Africa World Press, [2019]
Identifiers: LCCN 2019001761| ISBN 9781569026342 (hbk.) | ISBN 9781569026359 (pbk.)
Subjects: LCSH: Afolabi, Niyi--Travel. | Nigerians--Travel. | Travelers--Nigeria--Biography.
Classification: LCC CT2528.A344 A3 2019 | DDC 305.896/69--dc23
LC record available at https://lccn.loc.gov/2019001761

Contents

Prologue	vii
1. A Dream Deferred	1
2. A Divine Encounter	21
3. Mixed Re-encounters	47
4. Transatlantic Gulf	63
5. The American Journey	85
6. Contemplations	99
7. Negation of Nostalgia	115
8. Nostalgia Plus	137
9. Season of Samba	155
10. Song of Freedom	165
Glossary	181

v

Prologue

"O que escrevemos hoje será histórico amanhã"
[What we write today will become history tomorrow]
-Vera Barbosa

In multiple narrative voices, *Cosmic Whispers* weaves together the memories of two intimate characters whose divine paths magically crossed on the Brazilian side of the Atlantic. Not only did these two characters cross paths, but two countries also collided: Brazil and Nigeria. This is a ritualistic return to my African roots through cosmic whisperings. The plot is circular as it begins with dreams of greatness and forging of a family in love. The dreams suddenly become deferred; only to be further dislocated by the currents of life and the manner in which they parted ways. Instead of the perpetual fulfillment of deferment, they were rejoined decades later by the mysteries of life and dreams that lingered on. This story is a dialogic imagination in two movements. The first depends on the omniscient narrator to narrate encounters, dislocations, reencounters, sustained agitations, and critical commentaries. The second movement introduces the voice of Lúcia as she communicates directly with Clétus as well as with the (silent) reader. In the end, the magic of death snuffed the life out of Lúcia due to a terminal disease. This narrative is partly a celebration of her purposeful but short-lived life as well as a reflection on the fragility of life itself. On many occasions, the narrator exhumes socio-political and philosophical moments as an aside to the main plot, while also giving historical context to the narrative construction.

As the title suggests, the narrator becomes a metaphoric whisperer. What is being whispered is not in any way materially collectible. *Cosmic Whispers* unveils old and new memories that are forged in rare moments of magical activation and deepest meditations. They are enchanting mementos. Reality and fantasy often collide through mystical fragments and protracted extensions; instructing us of multivalent twilights—from the known to the unknown, from the tangible to the intangible, and from the concrete to the fluid. As the narrative compensates for deferred dreams, it also celebrates a woman for all seasons, who, despite the odds, gave all she could to her family, friends, and humanity at large. The narrator also interjects elements of semi-autobiography by sharing rare experiences of the American Dream's journey, the effects of paradise delayed, and the rarely shared intimacies of contradicting souls. The curious reader will gain insights into how inner wills defy social norms and structures; how innocence is lost forever and how in the process, experience empowers the naïve to fight for the sanctity of life. We will journey through São Paulo, Salvador, Chicago, Wisconsin, and Miami, among other locations in the Americas, and situate the narrator as an errant sojourner in uncharted territories. As Vera Barbosa noted in the epigraph above, "what we write today will become history tomorrow." If there is any universal moral, what has been documented here has in fact become history today even for generations yet unborn. We are all whisperers. Yes, we are all whisperers seeking opportune essences of our own mysterious inner harvests.

1

A Dream Deferred

Vera Barbosa
©Barbosa Archives

The August flower is no more. She unexpectedly succumbed to the chills of November. The news came as suddenly as it dissipated. It was painfully hard to bear. Such a heavy burden on my fragile and sentimental heart. The flower must have gradually lost her pristine petals of life in the midst of summer. Alas! It was not about the North American weather. She was uniquely Brazilian. The chills of November in the USA were still manifesting as summer gems in Brazil. For many days, I was in total shock and denial. How could such an angel vanish from our mother earth without any trace? Where is her abode now? And what exactly is she possibly doing there? Good hearted, affectionate, generous, strong, and affable—just a few of her attributes. She could make the most discouraged person brighten and lighten up with a new sense of purpose and hope. Lúcia was the embodiment of peace, joy, and tranquility. She was an inspiration to many associates who benefitted from her wide-ranging professional, administrative, and therapeutic services. A retiree who kept busy in her daily life by reaching out to others and helping them reach their human potentials without charging a dime. She was a selfless giver—a contemplator and a meditator. I knew her as a passionate cosmic thinker who had been schooled by the teachings of ancient philosophers. Her daily routine was to meditate and do Yoga exercises. In the midst of tons of chores: kids to take to school, food to prepare before they set out, even domestic animals to feed. She was such a strong woman, who faced many storms in life, but always resolved to find solutions against all odds.

Behind such an apparent strength and impeccable beauty, one can deduce hidden supernatural influences. She is well-read on the topic. She even had some of the emblems in strategic altars all around her house. Burning incense for them was a matter of daily ritual in her life. Her gurus were mostly

Indian: Sri Sarada Devi[1], Bhairavi Brahmani[2], Parahamansa Yogananda[3], Swani Vivekananda[4], and Maharishi Mahesh Yogi[5]. These were all considered divine inspirations to which she burnt incense and whose values she extoled. She emulated the discipline and principles of these Hindu monks. They were well-read, educated, and proficient in English; organized and positive thinkers. Their work has even been translated into Portuguese, and their books were readily available in Brazil. They all shared some pathways to the divine. The most pronounced teachings were the classic yoga pathways such as *bhakti* (devotion), *karma* (action), *jnana* (intellect) and *raja* (meditative practice). Some of these gurus see in transcendental meditation a way to engage celebrities such as the Beatles, Merv Griffin, Oprah Winfrey, Clint Eastwood, and Mary Tyler Moore, among others. Indian gurus to whom Lúcia subscribed her entire spiritual life sought to teach spiritual impulse to Westerners, an impulse that is engrained in meditation without compromising their sense of factual reasoning in history and science. Their essence of the Indian tradition was what Indians call *sanatana dharma*, or the eternal way, a science of

---

1   While there are several critical works on Sarada Devi, her own individual works are limited. See for example, Sara Devi, *The Gospel of the Holy Mother* (New Delhi: Sri Ramaknishna, 1984).

2   Though equally considered one of revered Indian Yoga masters in the West, has no book of his own but compiled teachings that are not available in print.

3   Regarded as one of the greatest thinkers of our time, especially concerning science of meditation, his works are numerous and illuminating as a major influence in the West. See, Paramahansa Yogananda, *The Autobiography of a Yogi* (Berkeley: Self-Realization Fellowship, 1998).

4   See for example, *The Complete Works of Swami Vivekananda* (New Delhi: Advaita Ashrama, 2014).

5   See, Maharishi Mahesh Yogi, *Science of Being and Art for Living: Transcendental Meditation* (New York: Plume, 2001).

consciousness, which has the potential to enhance the life of anyone, whether religious or secular—in order to ultimately deconstruct what it means to be who and what we are. Lúcia and I had a genuine dream—that of our being together as a couple at some point in our lives. Our ideals were alike in terms of professional drive but our spirituality was miles apart. She was the meditator while I was the intellectual. We could not really mix the two, for some reason, as I also had my own dreams that transcended the immediate passion between us. I had a goal to attain the highest educational qualification possible. She was content in her simplification of life and the belief that material accomplishments were terrestrial. I was relatively too young to agree with her, though we loved each other so much. She was older with three kids over the years, and for some reason, despite my inadvertent departures and arrivals, it felt as if I could not let go of her. The dream was deferred decade after decade and at some point, we realized it was not meant to be. As I regain consciousness and catch my breath after almost three decades, her family seems to have changed a lot. The kids are grown up and some are even married and raising their own children. The occasional opportunities to meet them were emotional because Lúcia is no longer in the picture. The news came quite unexpectedly. She had contracted gangrene in her foot and was battling terminal cancer. I could not understand why such a giving person could pass on to the beyond so unceremoniously. I reached out to her, via a phone call, at the University Hospital of São Paulo, where she had been admitted as a matter of emergency. The premonition was there, yet part of me was in denial. I thought of what could have been between us if things had gone right without the contours of life. I thought of the dreams deferred—and even the fact of our being separated by the Atlantic for a long while. I even contemplated the possibility that I could have returned to Brazil from the USA instead of completing my doctorate degree. I also weighed the decision I made to leave Brazil in pursuit of greener pastures in the USA. Though she was supportive of the journey, part of her wanted me to stay in Brazil. She was also not quite ready to take on the responsibility of raising an adult in the midst of the balancing act of raising her own children: at least two of which were from different men. I would have been the third man in the picture. It would have been a fleeting thing—the love notwithstanding. The love was not meant to be, I suppose. I tried to convince myself as a form of self-consolation in my reflective analysis. Perhaps the love was but an impulsive wishful thinking. Yet, the reality was such that I would have been a burden for the initial years of the relationship. It was not realistic. My focus was on my education and I did not have the funding from Nigeria to be self-sufficient. That would have helped the relationship somewhat. Due to my lack of financial support, I would have depended on the goodwill of Brazil and Lúcia. She must have had her own disappointments with men in the past, but she did not say much at that decisive moment. We just did not have the space and time to engage the issues exhaustively towards a successful resolution. Yes, perhaps it was not meant to be.

When I first met Lúcia at the University of São Paulo in 1982, it was in the naïve context of cultural and language immersion in Brazil. Though our initial encounter had happened in the "Circular" bus, the subsequent ones had happened at the "Bandejão" or Student Cafeteria where we had opportunity during her long lunch breaks to exchange romantic poems and talk briefly about life. It was not long before I realized she had a six-year-old child. Obviously, she was much older than I, but there was something young about her: beauty, vitality, strength, demeanor, charisma, and intelligence. She was an Executive Assistant at the Faculty of Architecture within the same university where I was studying Luso-Brazilian literature. Given that my stay in Brazil was as short as a semester and

France was equally beckoning to my group of seven students who had gone to study in Brazil, I felt an urgency to get to know her even more. She was equally pressured by her emotions and by her occasional visits to our condominium, located very close to the university campus in Butantã. One Saturday, without notice, she showed up at our residence. It was a mixed visit. It would have been a dream come true but for one thing. She came with a "boyfriend." I do not recall the name of that friend now, but it was quite upsetting. We were all very nervous even if we tried not to show it. The boyfriend had brought me a gift of Martinho da Vila's "Canta, Canta, Minha Gente"[6] (Sing, sing, my people). It was one of those melodies that filled the radios on Saturdays. It encapsulated for me the Brazilian *joie de vivre* as it narrates how turning to joyfulness would ultimately overcome the anguish of sadness. Brazil, despite many historical moments of brutality and sadness, has managed to overcome it all and escape in romance, samba and carnival. Though we never consummated our love, we maintained our deep affection for one another through communication and remained in touch for many years, even after my graduation in Nigeria.

I got to know the family of Lúcia because she insisted I visit despite my busy schedule as an exchange student. I did not even know she had a car because we had met on a bus. It turned out that she took evening classes to improve herself and also had ambitious dreams. It was a brief visit—overnight—but the whole family was curious about me and Africa; they also exuded a sense of solidarity with my subject of Carnival that was to be my senior thesis. Year after year, the connections deepened. First, letter writing and phone calls, and ultimately, returning to Brazil. By that fortuitous return to Brazil in 1986, just four years after we first met, a lot had changed. The young man, Sandro, was much older. While there was no longer any

---

[6] Martinho da Vila, *Canta canta minha gente* (São Paulo: BMG Brazil, 1974).

sign of a boyfriend, it seemed Lúcia had had her fill of men and was not as open to a new relationship as she was four years earlier. I was confused at the rather "cold" reception. I also understood that life was not meant to be so static. We all have our illusions and at times, illusions turned upside down become our realities. Lúcia got to see me at my weakest moment. I was no longer that rich Nigerian who could afford to live in a condominium close to the university campus. I was now looking needy, pitiful, and unsure of myself. The love was still there but rationality was more present on the part of Lúcia. She did not articulate it directly but from her actions and non-actions, I knew it was a bad time for me to try to reconnect. She discretely shared with me that some Africans in Brazil wanted to marry her to get their legal papers. She sounded very determined not to be used and dumped. She sounded quite smart and ahead of the game. She was absolutely resolved that she was not to be taken advantage of. In that rationality, I was the lone-standing buffoon. She did not propose alternatives. She did mention Bahia as a possibility but I knew I did not have close ties that could be any better than São Paulo. I was just so naïve and fresh in Brazil despite my earlier six-month sojourn. In the end, I spent two weeks with a Brazilian Professor of mine who took me in for a while and then I proceeded to try my luck in Bahia. Before my departure, Lúcia took me to McDonalds for a treat and to discuss our odds at love. It felt like the best place to eat in downtown São Paulo in those days. But I was not impressed by the restaurant or her. As a matter of fact, I was hurt that she turned her back on me at my most needy moment. Perhaps it was not meant to be.

 Beyond her reluctance to embrace my ideals and needs at the time, I felt entwined in a prolonged moment of a dream deferred. I sought solace and resorted to Langston Hughes's consolatory poem, "Harlem," to get a painful dose of reality when the poetic voice states rather contemplatively and emphatically: "What happens to a dream deferred? / Does it dry up / like a raisin in the sun? / Or fester like a sore— / And then run? / Does it stink like rotten meat?/ Or crust and sugar over— / like a syrupy sweet? / Maybe it just sags / like a heavy load. / Or does it explode?"[7] (Hughes, 1994 [1990]). In the context of Brazil, I did not explode. There were many alternatives that I was not aware of or that came to me so effortlessly. I owe a lot of gratitude to my past acquaintances and mentors, such as Professors Brandão and Santilli, who did everything possible to support my candidacy at the University of São Paulo's Department of Portuguese Studies. I was accepted as a "researcher" but without funding. I was also granted a free voucher to eat at the Cafeteria, pending the time I took the admission test into the doctoral program. Despite these efforts, I was not in the least satisfied. I felt waiting until January or after carnival in March to enroll for classes was a waste of my time, having arrived in Brazil in August. I felt I could be doing something else, somewhere in the remote locale of Bahia. I had no clue what possibilities were there, but was willing to try my luck. I proceeded to continue my life quest for meaning by leaving São Paulo for Salvador-Bahia. The trauma of a dream deferred could be intense. In hindsight, it may be easy not to feel the depth of pain that I felt then as I recall these memories in a different state of mind. I currently feel fulfilled as a professor, but looking back is as important as looking forward. At that moment in Brazil, my inner explosion was somewhat mediated by the fact that I had left a financially worse situation in Nigeria as the hardship was such that virtually every family member depended on the little I was earning as a junior professor. I had to leave that country where I could not see a future or where my future was truncated by the reality of social dysfunction. Something had to be done. Leaving was inevitable and Brazil

---

7   Langston Hughes, *The Collected Poems of Langston Hughes* (New York: Knopf, 1994), 58.

1 - A Dream Deferred

felt like the ideal place to reconstruct my present and strategize my future. The dream was deferred, but another dream was fermenting right by its side. I just did not have a clue where my destiny was headed. It was only a matter of time before I could decipher what was in store for my lackluster life.

I am not sure how dreams become deferred. It is as if its process is cryptic but its effect is the same. A disappointment that runs through the bones and you feel a sense of frustration and resentment. Dreamers are who they are because they have a profound yet elusive vision. When that vision is lost, they lose their inspiration and seek an explanation. "Harlem" was composed in the context of black American lives in the 1950s. Whether it is a historical poem or a philosophical one, the sting of life's positive possibilities being delayed is a universal pain. Langston Hughes compares a 'dream deferred' to a series of elements that have negative connotations despite the air of robustness, which then exaggerates the impact of their explosion: a raisin, a sore, rotten meat, a crust, and ultimately, a heavy load. Each element intensifies that potential explosion of a postponed dream. Along the lines of visual analogy, Langston Hughes sees a dream as a grape, which when newly born, is filled with vital energy. Yet, when the inspiration and hope are devoid of enthusiasm, the life energy is snuffed out of the dreamer. Frustration takes over the positive energy of dreamers and instead, replaces it with a permanent scar of failure. When dreams fail to materialize, they begin to weigh down the dreamer, sagging under the weight of a meaningless life. Likewise, when dreams are truncated, the dreamer seeks to confront the perpetuators of that deferment as a counter-measure to the potentially building explosive action.

In the historical context of the Langston poem, slavery had been abolished after the civil war. Though federal laws guaranteed the right to vote to black Americans, racial discrimination made such efforts at equality almost impossible. Segregation was the order of the day. African Americans felt marginalized and ostracized by White America. As one of the torchbearers of the Harlem Renaissance movement, Langston Hughes crafted this deferment poem as a response to the prevailing social injustice against black Americans. He suggested that when dreams are deferred for too long, they are likely to become a potentially explosive revolutionary act if not promptly addressed. Without a feeling of full citizenship despite emancipation from slavery, the sense of being second-class citizens after even serving in both World Wars, the denial of access to higher education and self-improvement, and barred access to public facilities, were all gradually mounting to a feeling of deep resentment of the American Dream that was elusive to black Americans.

Lúcia did not have to rescue me from a feeling of being a foreigner in Brazil. She also did not have to feel any compassion for my decisive resolve to stay back in Brazil in search of greener pastures—when I had consciously abandoned a professional job in Nigeria. It was a personal, professional and consequential decision. The analogy was misplaced but relevant. I felt as if living in Nigeria was like living under bondage and servitude because my professional dreams were not attainable in Nigeria at that time. I had to reach out to the shores of hope, elsewhere beyond Nigeria of the 1980s. I ended up in the hands of Lúcia who saw me more as a parasite than a partner or lover. While African Americans responded to racial discrimination through such a poetic outburst as "Harlem," Lúcia's mixed protest was more subtle than drastic. She had to guard against the explosion of her own soul that rejected my love recipe that seemed geared towards my own well-being and self-preservation. She was guarded and didn't accept my love because of her past experiences with men. She wouldn't open up and let her soul explode into another because she didn't want to get hurt as had happened in the past. Also, I felt she was doing this for my own good; my own self-preservation and not because she did not love and care about me. She needed to be sure of my intentions after four years of absence. It was a blurry moment. There was not enough time to explain things. For some reason, she chose to be cryptic rather than being direct. Perhaps out of not wanting to hurt me. In the end, both of us had dreams deferred that we had to resolve personally and differently. While she embraced rejection, I reached out for hope in other climes.

Hope was all that we had left, especially when all those around me seemed lost and confused. Reflecting on Lobsang Rampa's *Chapters of Life*[8] (1967), I came to terms with his idea of painting with words, when he postulates regarding lovers: "In the velvet-purple dimness cast by the shade of a tall pine tree, they stood together, telling each other only the things that lovers tell, planning the future, looking forward to Life itself… The night, beneath the harvest moon, was made for lovers. A night for poets too, for are not poems the essence of dreams and life?" Lúcia's choices were limited. She was without a husband and living with her maternal family and siblings, and struggling to make ends meet as a single parent who was also attending improvement classes to professionalize herself. I was not the ideal "dream" for her at that time. It was not as easy as I thought to pick up the pieces after four years of absence and rekindle the fleeting romantic love we had on the university campus of São Paulo. Even as I write this, the agonies of winter have passed and the promising birthing of spring soothes the spirit. Birds are chirping, declaring the goodness of God. The cycles of life remind us of the continuity of existence despite pain, disappointments, injustices, and other stressors. One is grateful to wake up full of hope and future expectations. As I listen to Jim Reeves I am reminded that there is a need to be grateful in all things. The country-romantic-gospel singer

---

8   T. Lobsang Rampa, *Chapters of Life* (London: Lobsang Rampa, 1967), 82.

proclaims in "We Thank Thee" (1962): "We thank Thee each morning for a newborn day / Where we may work the fields of new mown hay / We thank Thee for the sunshine / And the air that we breathe / Oh Lord we thank Thee.../ We thank Thee for the fields / Where the clovers grow / We thank Thee for the pastures / Where the cattle may roam / We thank Thee for Thy love so pure and so free / Oh Lord we thank Thee ..."[9]

Not only am I renewed, I feel a sense of peace into the future. As I contemplate the past hurdles of life, the hardships and injustices, the victories and conquests, I am reminded that life need not be all about failures and setbacks—that in due season there is joy in the morning. Lúcia brings back hurtful memories but also memorable moments when life was nothing but a glitter of gold. A dream may have been deferred but new dreams are surely ahead. New days are being born; new hopes forged. The future is lighted with a dawn of glory even if not immediately visible. Hope indeed was all that was necessary. Hope must not falter. It must be kept alive by all means necessary.

As I re-channel negative vibes of years past, recollecting them with the goal to re-purpose the future, I allow myself to dream again even if Lúcia is long gone to the beyond. I am not asking for a Lúcia reborn but a path towards inner healing, even though it has been almost a decade. I choose to unlock the dreams buried within the innermost self while overcoming the challenges of the past. Contemplating Lúcia allows me to escape the struggles of the moment, reach out to the positive moments of the encounter, the unfortunate moments of separation, and the settlement that led to a new vision of life. A phenomenal human being who may have been sent to transform the lives of others through positive thinking, she is a diva, a goddess, a transcendental figure who must be seen in her many symbolic representations. The more I contemplate her, the more I get

---

[9] Jim Reeves, *We Thank Thee* (London: RCA, 1995). [1962].

confused. Was she for real? Was she human? Or was she just a figment of my imagination? Why did we meet? Why not another person? Why Lúcia? When four eyes meet, there is always a cross-vision that penetrates both entities—a flash of the spirit that may make or break both entities as they give meaning to their chance encounter. Perplexed in my search for meaning, I reach out to Carl Jung to uncover my inner state of confusion and quest for meaning of my dream deferred. Jung talks of archetypal dreams and compensatory function of dreams. From my unconscious self, the conscious comes alive in the reclamation of my soul, dream, and elusive destiny. By enriching and restoring my vitality towards new dreams, the deferred dream is a prelude to integration within a new and harmonious future. How do I reconcile the conscious and the unconscious? Is this moment of deep reflections a sense of balance in the search for meaning of life? Lúcia is both real and existential. She is the mystery of my cosmic journey, a defining moment of growth, towards the transcendental being I have become.

I have often wondered about Lúcia's dreams. We had very few moments to interact even in the course of many years. Some of our moments were cosmic—through epistolary medium or via the telephone. It was a constant sacrifice trying to maintain a long distance relationship. A brother of hers, for lack of a better expression, called me a "playboy" for all he saw was someone who came briefly during summer research months to live with Lúcia and her family. He felt it was nothing more than a lover's fling, perhaps a relationship of convenience. He was angry at what he felt was the exploitative nature of the relationship. Of course, Lúcia and I saw it differently. How else could lovers see it? And more importantly, what were Lúcia's dreams? I knew she wanted to get pregnant. I knew we were not using any protection or contraceptive. I knew the love was such that we were free with each other sexually and the human product would have been conceived in love. But the fruitful expectation was not to be. Not enough time spent there perhaps or just a matter of biological timing? Whatever it was, mother nature was not on our side. I sometimes wonder what, if anything, that baby could have meant for both of us? Even in the family setting, I was also assuming a fatherly figure role but not a permanent one. Lúcia wanted to establish a family unit. That was obvious. It was for the moment a dysfunctional arrangement, but quite effective to the best of her ability. Three kids by two lovers were already a handful. Sandro. Fayola. Aisha. In that order. If she had gotten pregnant, I would have been the third lover and my child would have been the fourth, perhaps the second, the third? There was no way of knowing since I was never there for very long. The most I spent in Lúcia's household was a month. I always left for Bahia for research thereafter. São Paulo was a transit to a more culturally invigorating space which turned out to be my research focus: Bahia. The more I contemplate Lúcia's dreams, the more I am perplexed by her sense of positive magic. What was her magic that kept me glued for that long, perhaps forever? She is still in my consciousness. She is a woman of everlasting presence.

Lúcia is the buffalo woman. She is a special being endowed with strength, abundance, gratitude, and the air of the sacred. As a survivalist who is well versed in the teachings of the ancients, she is a symbol of survival. She often appears to me in my dream in moments of difficulty and distress. Oftentimes, she soothes the passing scar and prosperity tends to follow the ordeal; with the subsequent season of abundance and peace. At other moments, the dream may signify injury to the buffalo. In such moments, I meditate and pray for healing and guidance. It is usually not a moment to rush into decision-making. It is more of a moment of caution before entering into new endeavors. Lúcia had never appeared as a buffalo woman in despair in any of my dreams of her. Rather, she was always strong and in control.

Ambitious, determined, highly motivated and organized, she was a problem-solver who was a perfect match for persistent enemies. She was similarly diplomatic and yet a woman for all seasons who adjusted to situations according to the issue at hand. She can easily map out a schema for prefiguring the future even as she aligns herself with the unlimited possibilities of divine providence. World mythologies pay special attention to an extraordinary woman who is animated by divine forces. Widespread in folktales and myths, she typifies an archetype-heroine who protects an orphan-hero child. From Greek, Native American, to African mythologies, this divine female personality is steeped in mysteries of the oral tradition of epic proportions. She is an embodiment of the life force that is found in spiritual archetypes. While such extraordinary women are appreciated as exceptions to the rule, they constitute models that are often difficult to emulate due to the societal structure that keep women as second-class citizens, particularly before the era of feminist struggles.

Simone de Beauvoir's *The Second Sex* (1949)[10] offers one of the earliest statements to highlight women as oppressed by men. She cogently locates the origins of these profoundly imbalanced gender roles by arguing that women are portrayed by men as the Other; that is, in opposition to men, their oppressors. Considered a foundational text in the feminist thought movement, it caused ripples among adherents and critics alike. As an advocate for women's equal rights, Beauvoir contends that man positions himself as the center of being while the woman is considered insignificant and dependent on the man for her salvation. She is essentially denied her own humanity. In a consciousness-raising argument that ranges from "Facts and Myths," "Woman's Life Today," through "Woman's Situation and Character," Beauvoir deploys

---

10   Simone de Beauvoir, *The Second Sex* (New York: Bantam Books, 1949).

the disciplines of biology, psychoanalysis, and historical materialism to challenge the external processes that have been unjustly designed to stage the woman as an inferior gender. Questioning the different mechanisms used to justify her passivity and inwardness, Beauvoir argues that by denying her the possibility of independence and creative fulfillment, the woman is forced to embrace dissatisfying household chores of childbearing and sexual slavishness.

In other words, being a wife and a mother are imposed as social expectations to achieve ultimate satisfaction; and yet, instead of being the subject, she is indeed an object. Beauvoir's ultimate argument straddles between the economic underpinnings of female subordination on the one hand, and the economic exigencies of women's liberation, on the other. As a buffalo woman (as I see her), Lúcia may well be a contradiction when placed within Beauvoir's thesis. Yet, there are some correlations when it comes to her situation as a single mother and a homemaker whose satisfaction seems to be relatively dependent on external men even if she was completely in control of her household. What were the options available to Lúcia? She is independent to a certain degree as she can survive without a man but needs the warmth of a man—at least from the viewpoint of her actions. The degree to which she "needed" a man to complete her is debatable. The reality is that she was so independent that no man fitted the proverbial "wife and mother" role-fulfillment expectations for her. Could it be that she has always decided that her children were more important than any man? Could it be that she was better completed by her children than by any man? These are questions only Lúcia could answer. Overall, I see Lúcia as an embodiment of strength and pride—attributes that were well enshrined in the buffalo woman.

Despite her pronounced strength in the midst of challenges, Lúcia was also a retiree whose income was limited when it comes to taking care of a family of four with her meagre pension. The dream deferred for both Lúcia and I also had an economic underpinning as the 1980s had a particular impact on Brazilian society. Inflation, unemployment, and inequality were so rampant that they became a matter of daily readings and discussions in the newspapers and among the people. Brazilian reality had become one in which a blue-collar worker such as Lula and a black woman from the *favela* such as Benedita da Silva, had a real chance of being elected president of the Republic and mayor of Rio de Janeiro, respectively. Development models under authoritarian or democratic regimes have managed to maintain some democratic form of government through modernization processes though most have failed to resolve inherited social debt based on inflation.

Yet, while economic growth is encouraging, the mix of popular dissatisfaction with poor wealth distribution, the persistence of corruption, coupled with the weakness of the judiciary system, raise serious doubts about the social impact of such promising outcomes. The crux of the social crisis stems from the persistence of unemployment and inflation, which lead to serious inequalities despite an educated population. The result was that inflation widens inequality by pushing the middle-income workers into poverty. While education has an important role in determining inequality, it fails to account for the cyclical pattern of inflation and inequality in the 1980s. Ultimately, social inequalities in the 1980s are unrelated to changes associated with educational attainment. Despite Lúcia's educational attainment, her economic dream is directly truncated by the reality of inflation, which then reduced her economic power and moves her from a potential middle class citizen to a poverty line worker. As a consequence, Lúcia's deferred dream is a direct consequence of a larger Brazilian deferred social equality dream. After all, racial democracy in Brazil is still nothing short of a fantasy. If I were a person of financial influence, the dream of Lúcia and I may have collided. She chose aloofness because she had nothing to gain from the impending marriage of convenience. Simply put: Love was no longer blind.

I could also consider the deferred dream as the failure of a "convenience relationship" because I chose to leave Africa. Nonetheless, I departed with a sense of disillusionment. Only a year after graduation, I was out of Nigeria in search of greener pastures in Brazil. Love did not save the moment. Instead, like Lúcia, I was a victim of the drastic conditions that made me seek economic refuge elsewhere—outside of Nigeria—in pursuit of higher education. The era of the 1980s in Nigeria was a time marred by the symbiotic relationship between unemployment, inflation and stagnant economic growth. The justification for the inverse effect of inflation on price levels is that inflation was not responsible for aggregate demand pressure. Rather, it was due to instabilities in the supply chain of goods at both the domestic and foreign supply levels. Managing the relationship of inflation, unemployment and economic growth in Nigeria was a constant for suppliers and consumers. In fact, inflation and unemployment have been identified as key determinants in the underdevelopment of Nigeria in the 1980s. Despite the huge human and natural resources, the Nigerian economy was characterized by low per capita income, high inflation levels, unemployment, and many socio-economic challenges. Like a cyclic process, the economy continued to witness slow economic recovery, which was immediately followed by economic recession and depression. Due to the introduction of the Structural Adjustment Program (SAP), the ensuing depreciation of the naira exchange rate made it difficult for many industries to import raw materials and sustain their production rate. Just as it had in Brazil, the downturn in economic growth led to a huge rise in the poverty level.

Busy with work and family, Lúcia and I had little to no time to discuss my predicament. I was resolved to remain in Brazil in 1986 and had informed my siblings back in Nigeria that I was definitely not coming back in the near future. It was clear to me that the choices before me were between Brazil and any other country that would take me. Nigeria was no longer a choice based on the news about inflation and the structural adjustment program. I had to reach out to another dream; perhaps the American dream? It dawned on me that I had applied for doctoral admission into many Brazilian and American universities. I was also following up on that dream to the best of my ability. My circumstances made me contemplate Martin Luther King Jr's classic "I Have a Dream"[11] (1963) speech. The situation was different but the message was applicable. I too had a dream. Every word or sentence of that speech was carefully chosen by that man of God. It is so hard to cite from as its historical multidimensionality remains relevant even in the present. I cite but a few lines: "I have a dream that my four little children will one day live in a nation where they will not be judged by the color of their skin but by the content of their character."[12] As a black Brazilian woman, Lúcia was still a victim of racial discrimination. Likewise, as a young African in Brazil, seen primarily as an underprivileged Afro-Brazilian, I was equally a victim of racism. With higher education and social class, the treatment shifts a little but the reality of depravation remains constant. Martin Luther King Jr. got it right. Beyond the emotions, the facts cannot be faulted or denied. We are confronted here with two dreams; one deferred,

---

11   Martin Luther King, Jr., "I Have a Dream," Martin Luther King Jr., James Washington, ed., *I Have a Dream: Writings and Speeches That Changed the World* (New York: Harper One, 2003). 102-106 [1963].

12   Martin Luther King, Jr., "I Have a Dream," Martin Luther King Jr., James Washington, ed., *I Have a Dream: Writings and Speeches That Changed the World* (New York: Harper One, 2003). 104 [1963].

the other invoked for posterity. One is a lamentation; the other is an affirmation. In the crossroads that provoked this writing of permanent memories, I dedicate these reflections to that buffalo woman who is beyond description. Lúcia remains that spontaneity of the soul that refuses to be forgotten. She is a woman of presence. The cosmos will not be the same without her. She fulfilled my dreams even in her afterlife.

Vera Barbosa and Fayola Barbosa.
©Barbosa Archives

2

A Divine Encounter

Quilombhoje em 1990. Da esquerda para a direita: Abílio, Esmeralda, Oubi, Miriam, Cuti, Sônia e Márcio.

The Quilombhoje Collective (1990).
©Barbosa Archives

21

Cosmic Whispers

Vera Barbosa amidst writers of Quilombhoje Collective
©Barbosa Archives

Like chapters of life, some encounters shape our series of journeys. Life's journey is often cyclical. A beginning. A challenge. A midway. An end. A new beginning. Some mark our lives permanently. Some have so much impact on us that we never fully recover from the emotions. My encounter with Lúcia was one such event in my life. A profound performance that turned out to be destiny. August Flower I named her through a poem. But that was an afterthought. In her, I saw beyond mere beauty. She was special. She was supernatural. Emotions cannot describe her in totality. Words cannot even begin to capture the magnitude of this magic, this gift of life. She was everything Brazil promised. She was also the exception to the rule. In the first encounter, we did not consummate our love. She was not a figment of my imagination. She was real. She was flesh and blood. Even to behold her was a burden as I felt she was this goddess that needed to be worshipped. She was not the only woman I had met. Definitely not the only one in Brazil. From students to workers; from celebrities to just acquaintances; encounters come in different shades, colors, and tenors. Lúcia was that embodiment of a priceless jewel that translates into hidden showers of blessing. In retrospect, I would not know if I am making too much of it but something tells me this woman impacted my life beyond description. She presented herself as God-sent in her simplicity and depth. We met in a bus. An unusual place to meet, indeed. Before the bus ride, we had noticed ourselves at the bus stop. We observed each other. Our eyes became four in the proverbial sense of two people seeing through each other. I had assumed she was a student. But that was incorrect. As an Afro-Brazilian woman, she was not a normalcy in the Brazilian university classroom of the 1980s. Her species was to be found in menial jobs and at best as a secretary. That was the lesson we learned as a group of seven young Nigerians studying in Brazil. How could such an encounter turn fortuitous? It was more of a state of mind within the reality of racism in Brazil. The irony of the encounter is only lost to the buffoon.

The unusual bus encounter is one of those anomalies that the critical mind would want to interrogate. Why in the bus? Why not elsewhere? Why not at a party? Why not at a rally? Questions without answers. Yet, the bus is not as strange as it seems. In fact, in today's world, the bus has become part of the rapid transit system that we find useful at airports and urban centers. For a fast-growing mega-metropolis such as São Paulo of the 1980s, over 10 million people take advantage of this system. While the struggle to use the system is less pronounced on a university campus than in the more crowded city centers, the future of Brazil's urban transport mobility may be based on the bus. The fashionable subway system is simultaneously springing up in some Brazilian cities but it is no match for the bus system. Considered cheap and efficient ways to travel from one point to the other as fast as possible and conducting a huge population in one swoop, the "Circular Bus" as it is called in Brazil solves a major congestion problem during peak hours. Brazil's industrial revolution started in the 19th century. The subway was common in the 1970s; the same way the circular bus flourished in the 1980s. The rapid influx of migrant workers from less developed parts of Brazil, such as the Northeast, demanded new urban designs and innovative transportation systems. Architect Jaime Lerner was the brain behind this urban transport innovation. His invention of the so-called 'subway on wheels' helped to transport more than 50,000 workers back and forth daily in the 1980s. By the new millennium, over 3 million passengers used the system. Instead of the subway system in London and New York, the circular bus-based infrastructure is much cheaper to build than going underground like the metro systems in other global mega cities. Thirty-five cities in Brazil use the circular system. The circular bus is like having two to three buses in one. Such a high-capacity bus is capable of carrying 250 passengers at once, which eases the burden of crowding and delays to get to passengers' destinations.

The destined encounter with Lúcia happened on the bus of the century. Our eyes had met before taking the bus. Love at first sight they say. Her eyes were penetrating; her demeanor stylish, her hair long, stretched, and classy; her aura, a reservoir of charisma. I was sitting while she was standing. My eyes were glued to her. She was carrying some books turned inwards and I could not easily read the titles. She also had some school files. And she had a big fancy bag that hung by her left shoulder. I imagined she hoped to sit down to read briefly before getting to wherever she was going. I offered to hold the big bag for her. For some reason, I was reluctant to offer my seat. Not sure how I made that decision. I was confused about how the gesture could be read. I was also afraid of rejection. The Circular Bus rocked back and forth like a snake when it passed through a rotunda or campus circle. It was completely filled to the brim by passengers. It was the closing time and rush hour to get home, all combined. It was a free ride that took all students and workers to the entrance of the university. From there, most passengers took another bus. I was transported and arrested by her beauty, and by her sheer overwhelming yet graceful countenance. She smiled often; sometimes looking the other way and returning to take a quick glance to see if I was also looking at her or smiling. The romantic hide and seek continued for a while until I realized I had to strike up a conversation before it was too late. My African garb gave me away. I asked if she was a student and what she studied. She responded she was a worker at the Faculty of Architecture, but studied Tourism Management at a private university. That was not enough for me. I needed her phone number. I was not sure how to get it and how to justify the request. I quickly asked if she would like to have lunch at the Cafeteria someday. She responded affirmatively. I was relieved. I then asked if I could have her phone number. She obliged with a delight. I started imagining how to win her love. I was innocent in the ways of romance though I had had my share in Nigeria at the level of poetry writing. Yet, this was a very different level. Maturity was obvious, but it was still very emotional. We soon parted ways and I was so pleased that I had her contact. It was all I needed for that first mysterious encounter.

Even though I spent six months in São Paulo before going to France for another semester and then returned to Nigeria to complete my undergraduate studies, the time I spent in Brazil was a mix of curiosities, research, classes, joyful moments, countless encounters, and a singular memory of the impact of Lúcia in my life. For some reason, after her visit to the condominium in the company of her "boyfriend," I was so hurt that we only casually met at the Cafeteria with the understanding that someone else was in the mix. The triangular relationship did not allow for a growing of the passion we had.

That was 1982. Even four years later, despite letter writing and sustained communication, what seemed solid started falling apart. It would take that return to Brazil four or five years later to realize that the love was rekindled, but not strong enough to sustain itself. The only path left was Bahia. Bahia brought more complications. I was admitted provisionally like most places as a "special student" pending the selection exam into the doctoral program. Bahia was not an exception where a certain Judith Grossman felt I needed to enroll first as a special student and after a few years, attempt the selection exam. I disagreed with her, but could not articulate it directly. My energy propelled me to find alternative admission in Brasília (University of Brasília) which I got with a CNPq (national research center) scholarship. It was the beginning of a renewed sense of hope that will eventually transport me to the United States. And as they say: the rest is history. Not only did I gain admission in Brazil, I also gained admission into four American universities the same year! I opted for the University of Wisconsin-Madison. It was a painful decision I later realized, rather too late, after I had arrived there and not felt comfortable. I gave up the University of Indiana-Bloomington, the University of North Carolina-Chapel Hill, and the University of Minnesota-Minneapolis to find myself in a rather cold environment in sharp contrast to Nigeria and Brazil. It was not just the physical environment; it was also the racist disposition of the people around me. My solace came from Brazil. Lúcia was my consolation. She was the best thing that happened to my life of transition and professional growth at that time.

Atlantic communication was the way we reached out to each other. They were heart-to-heart spontaneities that will last a generation. One such communication took place mid-August. I was yet to arrive in Wisconsin, USA, but also had left São Paulo, Brazil. The contents were self-explanatory in their depths and specificities. Lúcia was summarizing our last mails or my letters that she was responding to in no specific order. It made for a perceptive understanding of issues and concerns between us even as we tried to maintain this strange encounter and passion. She starts by acknowledging how emotional she was, the need for her to be candid about her feelings to be with me in the USA, and the challenges against such innocent dreams. She stated that since she knew that I was leaving Brazil for the USA, she had been faced with the difficulty of writing since she was sad and always overwhelmed with emotions that she has had to interrupt the writing on many occasions. She referenced my letter of August 12, in which I had written with such profundity and wisdom; a communication that ended up giving her security and strength. Due to emotions on both sides, I had hinted at the possibility of her coming to join me in the USA in December. I was very naïve. She was, however, mature enough to address the concrete plans for such a trip. She first clarified that she will neither have vacation in December nor will she have the necessary discipline to save up for a flight ticket. She declared that it took her close to twenty years to secure a secretarial position at the University of São Paulo and the feeling of working with pleasant people was a rare opportunity she was not ready to forgo. In the end, she got philosophical—wanting to know where exactly I wanted to live my full life: in the USA, in Brazil, or in Nigeria? She was also curious how I was able to resolve the cost of traveling to the USA. She also noted a particular reflection in my letter to her: "What is more important is for us to love each other. Without love, even if we are of the same age, it does not work. Lúcia, there is always a difference and such difference could be harmonized through living together and mutual sacrifices." Beyond analyzing the emotions of absence and coping strategies, she invokes nature, my letter, and my photo as the therapeutic elements that soothe her pain and sadness at the realization that I was indeed leaving Brazil for the USA.

It has been six months since my arrival in the USA. This coincided with carnival celebrations in Brazil. I received a mail from Lúcia containing a mix of write-ups and magazine features—mostly connected with carnival and not so connected. The overall mood and tone was celebrative as carnival often offers a moment of ecstasy and relief from daily tensions. The cover note, written at 2 a.m., indicated that she had gone to a School of Samba, *Camisa Verde* [Green Shirt], had just returned and wanted to communicate with me. She expressed joy of the moment, dancing on the streets, in the midst of loved ones, freeing herself from the negative burden of life and being filled with nothing but happiness: "What a carnival you are missing! What a pity! So much happiness, unity, dedication, and love! Everything is here, in Brazil! I called you just now. Seems you are much happier now. I am happier too. Miss you!" The notes capture her reaction to my previous communication in which I had shared my frustration with my academic supervisor two weeks earlier. She was giving me a positive vibration as usual to counter all the negativity I was passing through. Another note, typed but brief, signed "Lúcia, Your Love," analyzes her own frustration about so much expressions of love and yet the pain of separation that frustrates our painstaking efforts to be romantic. "Such is life, such is life," she laments. She indicates she often reads the cultural supplement of the *Folha de São Paulo* newspaper, which publishes love letters from lovers, and often thought of us in moments such as this one:

> "Will we make news still? An example of dedication, honesty, and love, perhaps? Shall we succeed in surviving these our scarce feelings? Look, I love you very much, ok? I will do everything to be with you in July. I send you love, affection, peace and power."

Lúcia seemed to be following up on the intensity of feelings that kept building up in us over the months and across the Atlantic.

The need to see each other was mounting so desperately. December had come and gone and we realized July was just another possibility to meet in the USA since she will be on vacation. It was just a dream. In the same communication, she had included the lyrics of an *Afoxé* carnival group's chant, *Afoxé Ilê Omo Dadá Ogiyan* in São Paulo. The leaflet that is usually distributed to the members to familiarize with the next carnival in 1988, was an opportunity for Lúcia to tease me again about 1988 carnival and the extreme hope that I could just perchance be in Brazil to celebrate carnival with the rest of the family: she cited Márcio, her brother, Esmeralda, Márcio's girlfriend, Sandro, her son. She even teases: "Who knows, you could just be here in 1988?" It is interesting how months are becoming years in wishful thinking about a sacred reunion. The leaflet declares *Afoxé Ilê Omo Dadá Ogiyan* as the very first *Afoxé* in São Paulo, while inviting everyone to join them for carnival in 1988. The Yoruba-derived "chant" in the leaflet pays homage to Ogiyan, the great warrior of the historic city of Ejigbo in Nigeria, and who ended all wars and re-established peace. Though the words were hard to decipher even for the Yoruba speaker, the linguistic corruption over the years, leaves a few things to the imagination in terms of meaning: "*Baba epaoo epa / Oniku rewre epaoo / ... Orixá igigun e Baba motixaoro ... / Baba ibure*" [Father, we hail! / Good ancestral being, we hail! / ... Old divinity and Father of Secrecy / Father of blessings]. Adherents of this group dress in white with blue linings; in so doing, they also remind one of *Afoxé Filhos de Gandhi* in Salvador-Bahia. The last item within the mail envelope was a tourism clip from *Veja* magazine from January 7, 1988. Lúcia wondered if we could visit the Smithsonian, which had centralized 14 museums into one global Institute. It would have been a special moment to visit Washington, D.C. with her. Dreams, dreams, nothing but dreams… Dreams conjured up in true passionate love. Each communication with her brings me agitation, peace, pain, sadness, joy, relief, and dreams. A mix of feelings that makes a lover wrestle with aspirations and disappointments. A wealth of information that only in retrospect can be digested and duly analyzed over space and time. I owe this meditative process to the genuine love of Lúcia.

As much as Lúcia's communications brought some consolation to my disturbed mind in a foreign land, my own reflections about what I was feeling in a new environment were somewhat sacred. I use the word "sacred" in the secretive sense of inner feelings; in that I would rather hide these feelings from the public. These are intimate and profound sensations that were eating me up on the inside, while I was also trying to focus on my objectives in the USA. Yet, a significant part of me, a vulnerable part of my emotional being, was held captive in the hands and heart of Lúcia. Such intimacies are best shared only with one's lover, and one's lover alone. I wonder if I am not breaching the element of confidentiality on both sides by telling my story. But, I thought to myself: how else would others learn from the series of events that ended up scaring the living hell out of an innocent sojourner from a different world? My communication with Lúcia, dated September 1, 1987, sought to intimate Lúcia with my state of mind after a week of academic and cultural immersion in the USA. My letter complained about adjustment issues like registration, housing, and other necessary orientations. There was definitely an issue of culture shock and I tended to compare African and Brazilian warmth to the rather cold American mechanical lifestyle, structural advancement, and pragmatism. There was a brief reference to a shocking experience in Chicago upon my arrival in the USA, which had been detailed in a previous letter without a reply yet. I was offended by some American police officers who had rough-handled me, commented about my being a "monkey" and called me "stupid." These were psychologically depressing moments that needed the consolation of a sympathetic soul. Even in the 1980s, things were neither as saintly nor rosy in the land of the free and home of the brave. A follow up note dated September 22, 1987, revisited the hardships of the Chicago ordeal as if trying to exorcise the pain and reach out for some therapy. I was reflecting on the bestial nature of the treatment and how people could be that mean-spirited. It seemed as if these absurdities are now normalized. I was suffering from the psychological damage of the event and in symbolic terms, I was reliving it as a therapeutic outlet and venting. Even as I write this, despite it being 30 years ago since it occurred, the pain is just as real today. I am not sure how long I will recount the experience or when exactly the memories and the impact will dissipate. There was no telling when and it remains a confounding mystery. That type of behavior was a contradiction for a nation that claims all are born equal. It is an illusion. Racism is very much alive in God's own country.

    Following my initiation on racism in the USA, I became interested in all cases of racial discrimination. About four years after my arrival in the United States, I witnessed on TV the beating of an African American by police officers in Los Angeles. It was 1991 when the incident happened but the trial that led to the Los Angeles riots did not take place until 1992. It caught the nation in a standstill moment. Rodney King, who died in 2012, was at the center of the uproar. He was a victim of irrational police brutality that was documented by a controversial videotape taken by an innocent neighbor, George Holliday. The excessive use of force by the officers was put on trial locally (and globally) and unfortunately, the officers were acquitted. As a result of the injustice, the infamous 1992 Los Angeles riots erupted and lasted for six days, during which African Americans expressed outrage by disrupting social peace. Ultimately, 63 people were killed and about 2,400 were injured. It took a joint effort of the California Army National Guard, the United States Army, and the United States Marine Corps to secure peace. When it was all over, civil rights cases were brought against the four police officers for violating the civil rights of Rodney King. Two of the officers were found guilty and sent to prison while the other two were acquitted. Rodney King was awarded $3.8 million, but died under mysterious circumstances in 2012 after publishing a memoir. The King affair offers an exemplary case study on how the police can attempt to cover up their brutality without any supporting evidence. The videotape helped to highlight police brutality publicly and convicted the culprits through widespread public outrage. Meanwhile, the police attempted a cover up through intimidation and victim blaming tactics. This was an approach that backfired and exposed the police for their occasional use of excessive force. While there were not similarities between my racist treatment in Chicago and the Rodney King beating, I felt that I was powerless to pursue a case against the police because my situation was not high profile and I was a foreigner who had just arrived in the country. One can only imagine how many cases have gone cold or closed due to lack of political power, will, advocacy, and strong representation.

Racial discrimination, though full of negative feelings, is not the only issue that is fascinating in the USA. Discrimination affects the foreigner like a disease. With time, the same individual gradually learns to see beyond that stigma as a matter of survival and obligatory assimilation. Technological advancement and pragmatism were also attributes that prompted the migrant to adjust. In the course of the changes that I was going through and with the help of an interlocutor such as Lúcia, I started doing a self-analysis. In a communication sent to my Brazilian joy on November 6, 1987, I had divided my reflections into four parts: (i) Preamble; (ii) Before arrival; (iii) Arrival and after; and (iv) Immediate future. Lúcia had complained in previous communication that I was not giving "more precise news" as if time was not on my side and I was using postcards as an excuse to say fewer words. Compelled to say more, I decided to summarily analyze my state of mind. Due to stress perhaps, and the cold weather, I had also gone to the hospital concerning a flu-related ailment. That may have explained my slowed response to Lúcia's letters. I explained all this in my opening statement, but what did my "Preamble" entail? .Part of it went thus: Who is Clétus? Who is Lúcia? What is so natural about us? Who are we? This last question is more shocking. The truth is that we know each other well enough, but there is mystical sense that shapes our destiny—perhaps that was what led you to ask if I could just go "pluft" (disappear) or to express your inner fear about the solidification of the relationship just like any human being? I doubt if we can escape this destiny and what bothers me is how to take our situation concretely and name it for what it is. I appreciate the freedom you have given me to be practical and realistic and not make impulsive decisions for us out of the fear of losing me due to distance. At least, it seems as if it is not all clear to you yet. The uncertain moments I am facing here since arrival also make the clarity of my thinking questionable; yet I am still myself—we are who we are Lúcia, we are!

The second synthesis regarding "Before arrival" described our encounter in Brazil and its magic that remained a mystery to both of us. What does it all entail? What kept me strong and brought me joy was our "reencounter" soon after I returned to Brazil. Do you remember the day we met again at the Cafeteria? All of this may be seemingly "coincidental" but we both knew it could not have been per chance. I could have arrived and not found you; though I would have done everything to find you. Seeing you at that same venue was a positive signal. Besides, our communication changed in tone; from a sacred level through which we spoke by spiritual codes, through harmonizing our energy and hearts as true lovers. Thus, leaving Brazil for the USA was both desirable and undesirable. The dreams were so compelling in the sense of opening up new perspectives and possibilities for me that I could not let the opportunity pass. Nonetheless, the incident in Chicago paralyzed everything and made me regret even leaving Brazil by changing my vision of the American system. When it comes to the third synthesis as contained in "Arrival and after," it dealt with the crux of my crossroads moment. The Chicago scare was a key event that offset my entire dream of fulfillment in coming to America. I paid so much money to a defense attorney to defend myself, my studies were disrupted, at least temporarily; and I became somewhat uncomfortable and untrusting. I even created an internal self-defense mechanism. I was shaken up and there was no divorcing that from everything else. You can interpret my writing any way that you want, but I am flowing very spontaneously even though I know you are very sensitive. Yet, you are the one provoking me to let loose of all my feelings. How do I recover all that has been lost: time, money, honor, and impressions of others? Lúcia, I am carrying a burden that only the end of the semester would decode. These are my precise moments you have asked to share. The future is only a dream, a divine plan, who knows? Now, can you tell me more about your July visit?

Lúcia's request for a deeper self-analysis of my situation in the USA forced me to face the "before-during-after" predicament of leaving Brazil for the USA, and what that meant for us. It was a necessary but painful process of reflections. It brought out things I was not prepared to know about myself. It also spontaneously allowed me to face the predicament of the past, the reality of the present, and the probabilities of the future. November 11, 1987 was the date of her letter—indicating the proximity of the end of the semester as well as the coming of Christmas. She asked me to grow up and cease being a kid; discover myself and pay the price for my objectives was probably not what I wanted to hear from a caring person. I had to first thank Lúcia for this psychologic push to face reality. Then, I confronted the issues that I feel may affect subsequent letters from Lúcia, and I wanted to avoid that influence. It was out of my control. I addressed my helpless situation while in Brazil and the fact that she was not as supportive as she could have been. The analysis was making me less at ease as I had to address her role in my decision to pursue my goals, nonetheless. I felt candid discussion could affect her afterwards but she also asked for my candid opinions. She needed to know that I did not initially go to Brazil to stay, but to gain admission and later return after getting the necessary funding. When I was faced with competing with 45 Brazilian graduate students and I was among the 6 selected for gradate admission, this triumph gave me a sense of fulfillment against all odds. Even after all that success, I still gave up on Brazil and left for the USA. Yet, now that I am in the USA, I am complaining about everything as if I wanted things to be easy and without challenges. I ended up bursting into emotional tears as if I had touched on something that I did not want to address. I pleaded for her understanding and candor as I swiftly and abruptly ended the communication with the feeling that I had opened a can of worms. Regardless of the impact on writer and reader, I felt a sense of peace that the revelations were real and precise the way Lúcia wanted it. The question now is how she was going to react. I would never know.

A day later I was ready to write with a more relaxed state of mind. I was ready to respond to Lúcia's curiosities without mixed emotions and with clarity. Wishing her a Merry Christmas, and dated November 12, 1987, I acknowledged her role in keeping me on course; otherwise, I could have been in an even more profound crisis. She has always had that mysterious sweetness with which I was able to be calm under pressure. I recall her provocation: "*Chore Clétus, chore, porque eu também choro agora, chore... Desculpe-me Clétus se estou sendo dura. Acho que o meu papel de Deusa deve se transformar agora né? Mas é assim falando que com certeza vou ajudá-lo*"[1] [Cry Clétus, cry, because I am also crying now. I am sorry Clétus if I am being harsh. I think my role of being a goddess to you must change now, right? But only speaking like this will I surely help you]. I realized the self-analysis made me vulnerable. I was provoked. In response, I counter-provoked her through my realities and spontaneities. Could this action be counter-productive? Beyond the initial clarifications of my state of mind, I opened up: I am always busy with the burden of everything accumulating, deadlines to meet, and other preoccupations. Your letter is a permanent letter of reference and not a letter to respond to at once. There is so much to put in action, but it is hard, Lúcia, it is very hard. An example was going to the hospital with an infection in my chin. They did some blood tests and it all came back negative. The doctor said it was all stress-related and not an infection. They advised me to rest. I told them I needed to

---

1   Vera Lúcia Barbosa, "Flor de Agosto... Felicidade," *Cadernos Negros* 24 (2001), 95-101.

study more instead of feeling depressed and falling asleep all the time. I was told the secret was to sleep and rest as much as necessary. Thank you for your phone call this morning. You asked: "Are you doing very well?" It was hard to answer "well" or "very well." I am not sure where I am getting the energy to write. When you mentioned "nostalgia," I cried. But what can I possibly do? Somehow, you felt that I was no longer writing as often like before. I assure you there is nothing wrong. I am calm now. Just hearing your voice this morning sufficed.

November is gradually coming to an end and the cold weather, perhaps, motivated me to write a few postcards to Lúcia. We were always wishing to receive communication from each other. In recent mail, Lúcia not only complained of lack of communication from me due to pressures of the end of semester, but also talked about the health of her family, such as her parents and Sandro. I took it upon myself to address these emotional concerns since she has always been emotionally supportive of me as well. The first postcard sought understanding concerning my busy schedule and explained why recent letters have been brief and summarized. No time for details until I completed my end of semester's assignments. The title of my postcard to Lúcia was: "Strength, Lúcia! Strength! Never Give Up!" I continued… I tried in vain not to write but even despite my efforts, I can only send them tomorrow. I thought of passing by the supermarket to buy food. Tomorrow is Saturday. Still no time. All the time goes by so fast. Since you complain about real issues, I am compelled to respond. Then you apologize for complaining: "Desculpe Clétus pelas queixas!" [Sorry Clétus for the complaints!]. Never mind. This is in fact a moment for us to unite. I also have the need to be supportive of you when you are weak, when the world is weighing over you. We will surely make it, Lúcia!!! Until then shall we continue in this state of "departures;" when shall we reach "arrivals?" By the way, today in the elevator, an

American woman who had visited Brazil in the past gave me three kisses, saying: "That's for you to marry; because I will not get married!" I found it funny and ironic. I thought of you. You know what, Lúcia? Here, the mentality is that most people do not want to have their own kids, an exaggeration of course, as more people adopt children. Some even desist from having children so as to feel independent. They end up having dogs and cats as companions instead of children. Is it not funny? What do you think of my analysis? Not sure of how I will spend my Christmas alone... Missing you!

I now feel a sense of admiration for those who keep diaries. It is therapeutic. It frees the mind. How does one go over tons of pages and decide what is relevant and touching to remember or document? How many of those pages can be turned into reflections? The epistolary format of documenting memories is a little different, yet challenging. It is a dialogue. It involves someone else. Otherwise, the communication is incomplete. It is so lovely to read Lúcia's letter of December 6, 1987. She was responding to about 5 mails she had received from me over time—all written by me in November. I felt her overwhelming feeling of confusion of whether to respond letter-by-letter or summarily. She decides to respond letter-by-letter. Some of the lessons range from encouragement to take life seriously as opportunities come and go; and the moral that we must seize life's opportunities by sacrificing other things to achieve our objectives. In her usual intelligence, Lúcia states that it takes at least 20 years to grow up, 50 years to grow old, and many more years to live in harmony with nature and health matters. She consoled me not to worry about her complaints about writing less and to write as spontaneously as possible without constraint. On the issue of traveling to the USA, she asked for information about the best destination to connect to where I was living— such as New York, Miami, or Washington. Obviously, she was taking the July visit very seriously. But something crossed her mind to ask about my living arrangement: "Clétus, I still do not understand something: You live alone or with a family? I am referencing the person who attended the phone, I was surprised; or was it just an extension?" Of course, the person was my roommate. At that stage, I could only afford to share expenses with a fellow graduate student. Lúcia also queried why I do not talk about my family in Nigeria. Regarding my sister in Nigeria who wants to travel abroad, she says I should let her take her own initiatives and not depend on me solely as it never works that way. Overall, it is a series of responses to issues raised in previous letters that have no closure such as asking me to send a photograph of myself while dressed for winter and in the snow. These are things I do not think about… I guess for a lover, she wants to know every detail of my life to gain a richer experience given the distance and nostalgia.

Many moments are magical in Lúcia's letters. It is like reading pure poetry. She appreciates passionate mails from me, too, that are about her and that are often composed as poems for her. She wonders if in the future, we can put all these spontaneous outpourings together and publish them. That dream is being realized as I write. In these perpetual transatlantic dialogues, there was one moment that I found so touching when she states:

> "I am sure that every day that passes by I am becoming more and more dependent on you. I need you, your sensibility, affection, love, passion, words, letters, and the spontaneity of your 'special' inner self. I wonder what will happen if this whole experience should cease. There will never be anyone like you, not even close. You were God's error: He allowed you to escape from another Era (period) and you were born now, perhaps to keep me company, or for us to keep each other company. We both represent the Age of Aquarius…"

Lúcia reflects on the other postcards she had received in November. It was philosophical about life being beautiful despite its infelicities. She reiterates that life and nature are beautiful; and despite the odds of life from childhood through adulthood, the family, and the need to succeed, it is important to continue the struggle in order to help others even after winning. She adds: "For whoever wants to succeed in life, attain an objective, you are on the right track and this is beautiful, despite the sacrifices. You never lost your identity, your humility, your sensibility, your humanity, and your spontaneity. You are happy in spite of everything." Lúcia insists that I should be happy with myself and with God. Other people are sad for various reasons: Some because they are selfish; others because they do not have someone like Clétus in their lives. Concern yourself with humanity. Rather, let us concern ourselves with humanity together, ok? Never mind if I forced you to open up and tell me things from your inner being; it is all over now; no need to be ashamed... everything is in the past ... You had to react the way you reacted... but it is in the past now. It is fine for us to express ourselves as we naturally feel. No need to feel that I am using your words against you but that was not my intention or what I felt reading your revelations and confessions. As for your professor, send her symbolically to hell and have her stay there until you get what you want. Of course, you still need her for references; so all you can do right now is swallow your pride and play along. You are on the right track to attaining your goals. Just do not be deceptive with me; always continue to be sincere with me; never be afraid to express yourself.

Lúcia mentioned, as an aside to my racial profiling experience in Chicago, how white women rave about their conquest of black Brazilian men while chatting in the toilets or clubs. The general sense, often stereotypical is that: "'Oh, he is so in love with me. All I have to do is just signal with my fingers and he will come running to me like a dog... I am a white Brazilian woman, and they do anything I ask. They like rolling with white women.' I feel so disgusted when I recall

all of this each time I see a black man with a white woman, because I know exactly what these women say afterwards." She commended my decision to send the letters despite my reservations about my complaints about the sudden slow flow of mails. She felt I did the right thing trying my best to keep the communication alive. She felt we did well clarifying our doubts and ambiguities, given the long distance relationship. She digressed by commenting about the political situation in Brazil. It is speculated that President Sarney will remain in power for another year while gasoline prices are expected to triple, thus causing inflation. It is a complete mess. The educational system is even worse with students being promoted to the next grade without learning or knowing anything. The government's excuse for this policy is that young ones need not be traumatized by testing and the possible impact of failure. She was critical about a government that derives pleasure in governing an illiterate or semi-literate population. A population that does not know much and cannot be critical of the government since it is easier to govern a passive, unengaged population. She urges me to do everything to complete my graduate program and overcome the situation with my advisor, so that in the end I can get great letters of recommendation in spite of her. She encouraged me to also visit Nigeria more often. She felt she does know me well enough as she should and wishes I talked more about my family in Nigeria rather than focusing on humanity and professional development. She wondered why I do not relate more with other Africans. She also thought of one day going to live in Campinas with so many trees and natural ambience. She closes with expressions of homesickness and wishful thinking: "Only you can make me happy… I need you, I need your love. Oh baby, I feel so good." Mutual feelings of nostalgia. I miss her too.

It takes a special woman to dedicate a few hours of her precious time to focus daily on a lover across the Atlantic after spending 12hoursaday at work, school, and in traffic. To appreciate such a woman, one must have gone through sufficient characters in life to gain the richest experience that allows for a comparative assessment of the human nature. A woman who starts her communication with "everything is ash without you, it is so empty and the night has no meaning… where are you, call me, call me, call me, we hardly get to see one another, magic in the absurd…" is not an ordinary person. A woman who dissects one's solitude and does everything to provide strength and solace has a special place in one's heart. She is a natural encourager, a protector, a divine blessing who seeks nothing but the best for one's life and future. As I begin the closure of this chapter on divine encounter, it dawns on me that this is an endless journey. It may have had its specific moment of intensity within a sustained period, but it is so profoundly impacting on the spirit that I cannot possibly let it go without giving it meaning, value, and perspective. Only a special woman seeks to understand her place in one's life. Here is Lúcia dissecting her own thoughts and mine when it comes to her curiosities about who she really signifies in my life:

> "Our communications, the issues they raise deal with solitude, work, life, poems and issues of being your lover. Concerning being your girlfriend, I cannot be upset because I do not have the right to repress your freedom and necessity to love. I do experience jealousy, that's true, but I also have my rational and human sides. However, I leave it to your choice, what to do and who to love, because all I want is someone close to me, as long as this person is sure of wanting to be with me. I cannot question any of your actions. I also cannot cease to express my rare feelings these days. You are the one who must decide if you value them or not."

As direct as these reflections are, they also betray the inner spirit of the thinker. When it comes to work, Lúcia deploys the pressures of her own work as an example of necessity for fulfillment. By doing well in her work, sacrificing her time and often working extra hours to complete projects, she feels it is all a form of investment in future opportunities. She asserts the same thing about being in school and getting an education. By being strategic in completing one's assignments, diligent in one's daily assigned readings, and focused on set objectives, this process ultimately leads to fulfillment as well. She believed that anything less means one is on the wrong course and no one achieves anything in such a state of absolute confusion.

A closer look at this communication reveals some insecurity on her part, too. Perhaps it was the fear of losing a loved one, all of which may emanate from the fact that a female answered my telephone in the USA. It was an error in judgment by my roommate's girlfriend. Nostalgia may be what is at work here. Emotions could also be another point of contention. Lúcia enters into a deep reflection as if wondering if this Atlantic communication was just an illusion, a phase, or a dream that will soon disappear like a figment of one's imagination. She sounds like a lover feeling a sudden sense of loss and separation; of uncertainty. It is a passing moment of weakness that may actually be a true betrayal of love and affection. Lúcia seems to be preparing herself for the worst scenario, within an absence of just five months, with the advent of Christmas and Carnival, and with an imaginary woman she thinks may be in the picture. Painfully going round in circles, she makes her point known that she was scared, at least that was what I read from all of the mixed messages:

> "Determine what you want, my loving heart. Write poems Clétus, every time you feel the desire of doing so. We will publish them. Cry Clétus, any time you feel a knot in the throat. Speak your heart with the one who loves you and that you love in return. Be spontaneous with the person with whom you have confidence and whom you love so much. Only you know how to love. I wish you nothing but love.

You deserve having people who understand you in your life, those who know how to value you and your pure feelings, so rare, even inexistent in this age of chaos, of the end. Even children who were once the purest beings like angels, are no longer reliable, loving and selfless. From being angels, they have become nothing but *devils!*"

These are deep emotions. They can only be lost to the dispassionate. Even when we proverbially say that love is in the eye of the beholder or that love is blind, there is something inherently true in these sayings. While I cannot judge these emotions, they are indices that there are internal agonies and conflicts that are emanating from nostalgia. The mind can go, rightfully so, in many directions when it feels a sense of insecurity, uncertainty, and doubt. Love could be a beautiful thing… It also could be a hurtful thing when it loses control in the name of love.

My muse concludes with another provocation as if inviting yet another dialogue. Each provocation leads to other confessions and revelations about the depth of love and commitment. They all serve as a coping strategy to console hearts that are deeply in love and yet separated by the mysteries of the Atlantic and passing stages of life. She wonders what she represents to me: a friend, a lover, a girlfriend, just anyone, a counselor, or a consultant. Epithets that I simply do not distinguish one from the other. Emotions return as Lúcia offers new perspectives on how to overcome the odds against destiny of being together in love. She delves into an emotional state of philosophizing as she sees me in a metaphoric cage filled with blood-thirsty wild animals like the human beings of this strange planet. She prays wholeheartedly that I do not end up being contaminated by such a world of technology, inhumanity, coldness, diseases, and indifference. She laments the possibility that I will not be able to spend next Christmas, New Year, and Carnival with her family. She dreams that it is only going to be for a short while.

2 - A Divine Encounter

She prophesies that this will only be a phase and that I would do everything to ensure that it passes quickly so as to wake up into our new destiny. There is still a feeling of concern about the future. She apologizes for not being able to write more. She confesses an inner feeling of sadness in thinking that she may one day lose my love. She worries that with time, I may end up loving someone else. If that is the will of God, she promises to let go. She then cries in anguish for she feels she depends on me and that is a fact she cannot possibly hide. It is a mutual feeling that is, however, blinded by love. She feels she will never meet someone else just like me. Such are the spontaneities from Lúcia and me, as we face a destiny that continues to have its own endless twists and turns.

Aisha, Sandro and Fayola.
©Barbosa Archives 2000

Cosmic Whispers

Vera Barbosa
©Barbosa Archives 1986

Fayola and Aisha
©Barbosa Archives 2018

3

Mixed Re-encounters

Sandro and Márcio
©Barbosa Archives 2015

Encounters sometimes have their reencounters. One hopes that a divine encounter is never denied its potential reencounter. To be memorable, most encounters must have been positive. Some reencounters are not always pleasant but we only discover their significance much later—with the accompanying passage of time. There is no projecting what these reencounters could offer. Their subtle compromised possibilities often become a buyer's remorse after the fact. For four years, I had looked forward to such a reencounter with Lúcia. The opportunity came in 1986. I had left Nigeria with the hope of gaining admission into a Brazilian university and returning to secure sponsorship from my university where I was teaching and researching. I was a young lecturer without much opportunity for professional development in Nigeria since there was not a graduate program anywhere in the country that could enhance my career development in that specific field of Brazilian Studies. My first stop was São Paulo. University of São Paulo remained a positive experience and memory from the first time I was there four years earlier for language and cultural immersion. I had a few professors that I do remember: Professor Roberto Brandão and Professor Santilli of Languages and Literatures, and Professor Queirós of the Department of History. There were other acquaintances that invested their precious time to orient me while I was in Brazil. Lúcia was such a kind soul. We had maintained communication for a while in Nigeria but the cosmic relations soon waned with the pressures of life. Yet, back in Brazil, she was the first person I looked for. She was happy to see me and was quite eager to know what had brought me back to Brazil. I informed her that the plan was to stay once I gained admission and return to secure sponsorship in Nigeria. To my shock, once she learned of my intentions she was unusually indifferent and cold. While she had doubts and was no longer as impressed or invested emotionally, she was at least equally open and supportive—Just not as forthcoming as she was in our initial encounter. I know that was normal for a relationship that had spent four years in a constant flux. I wished I had maintained the contact and not just waited until I needed her assistance. Is this reencounter meant to be? I will soon find out.

Lúcia and I had lunch on a few occasions in the same Cafeteria like years past. The conversation was not as vibrant because there was a part of me that was not as joyful as before. I was preoccupied with what was going to be and if I had enough time to get all I wanted within the relative short amount of time I had left in Brazil. I was soon to find out that the admission process takes place in January before carnival and school started right after carnival in March. By my calculation, if I was returning to Nigeria, the admission must happen quickly but there was no such exception to the rule. It dawned on me that I had to change my plans. The mix of the timing of my arrival in Brazil and financial recession in Nigeria conspired to disrupt the admission dream I had in mind. The introduction of the so-called Structural Adjustment Program (SAP) in Africa, with a particular focus on Nigeria, led to the imposition of economic reforms that led to the collapse of manufacturing and agricultural industries. The consequence was a heightened unemployment and overall social insecurity. The Nigerian state failed as we knew it; as governance became impossible due to rampant ethno-religious conflicts that further led to protests by the Nigerian labor sector. The consequences were many: labor movements became active and disorganized; sporadic industrial strikes affected economic development, and ultimately, the SAP initiative led to an identity crisis, economic crisis, and the wanton desire by the educated elites to flee Nigeria for greener pastures. It was in this context that I, too, left Nigeria. On the Brazilian side, inflation and economic stagnation led to economic reforms that introduced a new monetary plan such as the *Real*. Despite the artificial growth related with future behavior of inflation, the economy only grew at 1.25% per annum, forcing the per capita income to drop to 7.6% during the mid-1980s. Overall, the economic situation in Brazil led to increased misery and social inequalities. This was the circumstance of my initial reencounter with Lúcia. With this background, Lúcia was also managing to stay afloat economically though we did not have time to discuss such details. Love became impossible in the midst of personal and economic crises. All I left Nigeria with were my academic credentials and a little less than $100USD. That could not possibly last me for too long. It was a desperate moment. I needed a miracle to make the impossible possible.

Lucia's reluctance to embrace my new reality was understandable. She was completely confused but not fooled. How can a lover disappear and reappear four years later without any notice? She also did not have enough time to analyze or rethink the circumstances. My airline ticket had a pre-planned two-week stay in São Paulo, which was not a lot of time to make things happen, anyway. She neither knew the details of my plan; nor did I know the details of her own life since I left Brazil. I basically assumed we could rekindle the relationship while making sense of my new situation if that was meant to be—staying on in Brazil. This was a frustrating moment for me. I had no money to propose eating out or having any pleasurable activity. Rather, I was needy and dependent. From afar, I was analyzing the aloofness and wishing things were different. I reconnected with a few friends. I also reached out to my former Professor of Brazilian literature. The latter was more sympathetic to my plight. A friend had paid for my stay in a hotel for three days but that was the best that person could do. In-between those three days, I was lucky to have a heart-to-heart discussion with Professor Brandão who arranged to pick me up at the hotel. I ended up staying with him for two weeks. During those two weeks, I had a chance to discuss both the past and present with him. We talked about issues in Brazilian literature and my new interest in focusing on Lusophone African literature. I also had an opportunity to interact with his rather young children. He had mentioned one of his older children was studying at the University of Texas in the USA. Not much was entering my head as my goal was to be admitted and be able to return to seek sponsorship. It was a gigantic gamble. But without such risks, one can never know what is possible. Despite my own internal frustration, the landscape was beautiful and encouraging. The environment at the University of São Paulo's campus was somewhat different from the atmosphere four years ago. Instead of the usual groupings of Africans by country, I noticed a rather small group of Africans congregating here and there. I wondered what had happened to the many students who kept coming to Brazil for their education. I was later informed by the few African students that the university took a drastic decision a while back to curtail admission of African students, after some were found to be trafficking hard drugs. This was quite disappointing and shameful. It made the rest of us look like members of the same unorthodox gang. It was a sad revelation that felt like a rude awakening as the African student presence I used to appreciate was now a wishful thinking. A thing of the past. How times change!

Despite these negative vibes, I was not discouraged in the least. I tendered all the documentation and references I had for admission to both African and Portuguese Studies. The outcome was not completely satisfying to me but at least gave me so time to catch my breath and not lose total hope. The processing resulted in provisional doctoral admission into the Portuguese Studies Department since African Studies was only a Center. Though I had that temporary acceptance as a researcher, I had to wait until January to submit to the annual selection test for admission. The idea that I had to come back to São Paulo or even leave the city was not exciting to me. São Paulo was not quite invested in black integration as Bahia, but it had enough activists to make the place conducive to learning. Lúcia was on my mind but I had given up on prospects since our conversation was more directed towards philosophical reflections. Two weeks went by so fast and I found myself on the way to Bahia with the hope that Bahia would hold better luck for me. I left São Paulo with mixed feelings. A part of me felt like it was an unfinished business, but another part of me was more frantic that departure may be without my return. The pain of leaving Lúcia behind one more time crushed my spirit. I was troubled by what was ahead but had no choice but to proceed in my quest for the purpose of life. Fortunately, Salvador, Bahia's capital city, welcomed me with open arms. Pelourinho, Salvador's famous cultural center, became a constant place to visit to enjoy daily musical and cultural gyrations. It contains the largest assemblage of colonial architecture in the Americas. The exquisite center boasts paved streets and vibrant colored houses with red-tiled roofs, which resonated in the kaleidoscopic and multiracial community. Antônio Carlos Magalhães, the then mayor of the city, had secured $105 million from the Inter-American Development Bank to rebuild Salvador as a Latin American cultural patrimony. I was fortunate to work on translation projects with the Franco-Brazilian photographer and ethnologist Pierre Verger (1902-1996), who settled in the city and documented local traditions such as the syncretic, African-rooted religion of Candomblé. In addition, the Federal University of Bahia was able to help me process my visa and admission yet I was still not satisfied. I eventually went to Brasília for better opportunities.

    Departure to Brasília was not without its own romantic mystery. Within a year of Bahia's rediscovery after four years of returning to Nigeria, I found a notsocompatible romance with a young woman, who was sadly not of the same education level. Initially, that was not a problem but we could not hold any steady conversation as I did with Lúcia. Márcia was mostly quiet. We had many fun moments, of course, and she was articulate in her own way. She was curious about Africa and seemed to harbor lots of negative stereotypes about Africa that were difficult to overcome except through a sense of humor. The beaches of Salvador provided an ideal setting for the curious tourist as I saw myself the second time around. Though I was living in Salvador, I was not firmly rooted as I was not quite satisfied with my life. My dreams and the years were passing by before my very eyes, and part of me wanted something different, vital, and better. Bahia opened up a new world of political and cultural activism to me via the Afro-carnival organizations. I had studied them cursorily as an undergraduate and started observing them even more in-depth. They mostly performed at the Pelourinho cultural center and gave a sense of a political energy despite the mask of cultural performance. The Verger translation work gave me enough to survive and I was learning quite a lot about African-Brazilian dynamics and relations from the projects. My fleeting romance with Márcia took a sudden turn. It took nine months to discover that a baby was waiting for me in Bahia after I had left Salvador for Brasília for at least six months. She was quiet throughout. Strangely so. I quickly arranged to visit Bahia to see the baby and returned to Brasília almost immediately. It was a painful experience. I had nothing concrete going on for me in Bahia—hence I could not be where I was not making progress. It was important to be where I was making some career progress even if it was symbolic. Mixed feelings. Painful adventures.

Living in Brasília had its own challenges. It was an artificial setting without friends or close associates. Emmanuel, a fellow Nigerian studying architecture, came to the rescue. He offered me all he could in student accommodation and ensured that I was satisfied when it comes to basic necessities of life. School soon started and I was eating at the Cafeteria for almost nothing. When it came to my studies, my psychological imbalance made it difficult to perform my daily duties. I was homesick and in emotional distress, and that made it hard to concentrate and focus on my studies. I missed home despite the need to exit from what I saw as a 'house of hunger'[1] even before I left. I also missed Lúcia despite her rejecting my advances in São Paulo. I struggled to focus on my studies even as I continued my quest for a better life, perhaps in the USA. I remained in communication with a number of American universities. I felt I had nothing to lose depending on what happens in Brasília. I was admitted with sponsorship at the University of Brasília. There was however a condition to the financial process. The funding agency only paid after three months of registration and classes which created a problem for cash flow. In the midst of this absurdity, the stress was giving me more impetus to think outside of Brazil. Leaving Brazil was such a miracle. I did not have the funds even after the admission came, but somehow the visa was approved effortlessly. Attempts to reach out to Emmanuel, a Nigerian architect-friend, and his associates for help proved abortive. They were strangely nonchalant. Such is life. Many reassured me that it was already a lost opportunity no matter what I did, but I refused to give up. Miraculously, a total stranger with the heart of God, encouraged me to reach out to his church. Reluctantly, I did just that and it worked. With close to R$3,000 reals in my bank account, I was able to make the arrangements and off I was on my way to the USA. Lúcia was also a financial contributor though she felt it was so insignificant. To me, the fact that it touched her heart to even help was more than significant. She was such a blessing to my soul. The chapters of life are taking their shifts and turns as I heed the call of destiny. Lúcia was my last intimate contact in Brazil and our communication was to become a powerful tool

---

1 Dambudzo Marechera, *The House of Hunger* (Illinois: Waveland Press, 2013). This is an invocation of Zimbabwe as an impoverished nation by the author, about the same time I had left Nigeria, a country that was also suffering from economic recession. I found a commonality in the impact of neocolonialism on both nations at the time I left home in my troubled prime.

3 - Mixed re-encounters

of restoration and regeneration. For decades, she remained a vivid part of my poetic spontaneities.

Memories of Lúcia are echoes of a time in history. A time when perfection was not an ideal but true emotion of love and care sufficed. They were priceless moments that can never be regained or truly recuperated. Appreciated for the way they held the soul intact as the contours of life took their turns. One would never know what the aftermath could have been in such moments of agitations, frustrations, and uncertainties. The words of encouragement and solace were necessary for keeping the soul alive. The short-lived experiences of São Paulo and Brasília were compensated by the powerful cosmic messages contained in the communication between Lúcia and me. They were memories locked in the mysterious pages of life. Memories truncated by the passage of time. Messages recuperated by the desires of gratitude for such a singular human being. Her most recent message came in early February of 1988. I already have a whole semester behind me. A new semester was on-going. I was better settled to the system and culture. It was Lúcia's turn to share her mixed feelings about life. Frustrations and joys. I was looking forward to news relating to carnival but what came was not close. She has missed the registration deadline of her graduate program and was wondering how she could manage all her expenses without a scholarship. She had gone there on January 7 only to realize that the registration closed December 22. She had cried a lot for missing the deadline as she hoped to find a way out to no avail. She needed to talk with someone and decided to communicate with me. It was so hurtful that she could not even share the bad news with her mom since she would be so sad and upset as well. She wanted to save her all the suffering over her daughter's progress. She talked about her brother, sister, and sister-in-law visiting them at home and everyone feeling in a festive mood. This festive mood in the household overshadowed the negative news about missing the registration deadline.

As a digression, Lúcia wondered naively why I could not join the family in Brazil and celebrate. She stated it was all a provocation to see if I truly knew what I wanted for my life. I did not know what to say. I had assured her that I did not plan to let the pressures force me to abandon the program and I was resolved to stay focused. She stated very emphatically:

"I liked it when you told me on the phone that you could never abandon the program half way. That is the idea! It is not a good idea to withdraw from the program. You must do everything to resist the temptation to let go. You should also try to reduce the course load. I am sure you will succeed."

Such a note of encouragement soothes the spirit. She had woken up as early as 5:30 am in order to prepare her child and herself for the day. By 8:00 am, she had arrived at work to ensure that she typed my letter first and send it off by the end of the day. Inviting me to join the festivity in Casa Verde Alta (Upper Green House) brought back memories. A district of São Paulo, located in the northern zone of the city, with an area of 7.1 km², and a population of close to 80,000 inhabitants, the locality boasts of an average monthly household income of R$ 1,400 ($365).

Primarily a mixed middle and working class population that transits between the region of Santana and the Garden São Bento, it is considered one of the noblest neighborhoods of the northern zone. Though the region has no Subway station yet, the district has easy access to the Palmeiras-Barra Funda Station and to the Santana Station. The district also has a bus terminal, known as Terminal Casa Verde, located at Engenheiro Caetano Álvares Avenue. Though I miss the family house, the demise of Lúcia does not motivate me to return to São Paulo as often as I would like. I always find excuses not to go due to negative memories of this unfortunate demise. Eduardo Luiz Trindade street is typical of narrow close-knit streets in Brazil where residents knew each other. Neighborhood dogs often congregate at night as if holding an assembly, barking loudly and gesturing uncontrollably to assert territory and predominance. In the end, the initial harassment is resolved with a sense of camaraderie and warmth. The community feels safe with this presence of animal protectors, speaking a whole different nocturnal language.

It feels good to process the deep emotions of Lúcia as translated from her expressive words. Her December 3 communication, received rather late in January is an example of such mixed emotions. She started with a request that I never stop this cosmic communication. For someone who likes to write, she feels she has met her God-sent match. She is grateful for this gift of writing between us: the care and affection. She praised all my communications to date and called them "beautiful." She appreciates such mutual attention, affection, and fulfillment. Above all, she feels she is the happiest woman in the world to be able to follow my career trajectory. I am also without words to appreciate such a sensitive woman that is beyond description. She poeticizes so freely in her deepest reflections: "I feel like a different woman from whom I used to be. You succeeded in transforming me, because, as I said in previous communication, I was already giving up on humanity; I was entering a critical existential phase without any perspective on the future." Instead of praising me for my personality, I feel she deserves all the praise. She is an angel, full of light, someone who appeared from behind a divine tree and fell right on my path with her smile, her expressive eyes, her tranquilizing voice, her loving gestures and her therapeutic body so full of warmth. Her communication is full of many queries as usual. She asked about my flu-related infection, stress, and if I was taking vitamins. These are rhetorical questions that are better left until my own future communication. She feels redeemed that I am talking less of stress and much in control of my challenges. She wanted to know if there are black people in Wisconsin and why I was not talking about or taking pictures with them. She feels fulfilled that in some magical way she is playing a vital role in my divine purpose. She suggests that I find a way to cope with the pressures of the professors so that I can move on to the next stage of my professional development. Homesickness is at work in what seems like an endless state of emotional flux.

Between November and February, winter is gradually rising to its chilly heights. Lovers of the cold weather may celebrate snow and the beauty of a white Christmas, but those from warm climes are not impressed at all. Lúcia wishes that her words could warm me up a little during the winter months. Fully desirable, and yet, wishful thinking at best. She was responding to two different letters but not the traditional way but below the pages as if summarizing her thoughts and responses. She felt that with time, we would both get to know each other better: our fears, our wishes, and our insecurities. She lamented her occasional sense of seeing me as a "wild man" based on my reactions to some of her provocations regarding my revelations and spontaneities that she was later using against me, such as a visit with my professor, who is 70 years old, to the Milwaukee Zoo. The visit was in the company of two other foreign students and Lúcia misread it as more than a casual visit. She pleaded that instead of getting wild with her for misreading the circumstance; that I should rather promise not to cease from being spontaneous and loving her. She confessed she had no intention of hurting or upsetting me. Rather, she pleaded that we continue to be respectful of each other; sincere with each other, and avoid hurtful words that cause anxieties. Lúcia reiterates the fact of being a human being with animalistic instincts—thus, quite normal for her to react to attacks and threats. She confesses that she has been cheated upon many times and been betrayed and hurt. As a result, her misinterpretations of the Zoo visit derive from past experiential fears, sadness, deceptions, and hurt. With so many feelings at play, the end of one communication leads to the beginning of another. No end ever in sight. The thought of a professor being one's lover is far-fetched in the American educational system. In Lúcia's logic, the female professor is right there with me while she is so far away. Why would she not be jealous of her? It is human nature. I completely agree with her apprehensions, though they were somehow uncalled for. I had no reason to cheat on her. That was not even an issue. My focus was surviving the first year of adjustments to a new environment, not a romantic escapade with a professor.

Lúcia predicts that one day we both will be nostalgic of these precious moments. She is as correct as ever. Nostalgia is central to these spontaneities. It is now a matter of habit for her to respond on the pages of my own communication as if keeping the transatlantic dialogues alive. She identifies transcendentalism as a characteristic in my personality. How does she perceive my person so accurately and not hers? It is indeed an irony that her first message was that she wishes she could win a lottery, so as not to work this year and be able to afford schooling without having to work as well. That is the extent to which rest is necessary to maintain a sane and productive mind. She realizes she works at times for over 12 hours on some days—including deliberately forgetting to have her lunch break in order to get the work done. That is the extent to which she is hardworking and yet feeling unfulfilled. She writes: "You know, it is a weakness of mine, acquired from having had many negative experiences! I am sure God and you will help me, love me, and rescue me in this sense." Digressing quickly as her fragmented responses seem to function lately, she talks about me buying a television so that we can watch it together but not for a long time. Rather, she prefers that we listen to music and enjoy ourselves. There is need for human contact, human dialogue, human expressiveness, non-verbal communication through the eyes, through the body, through the mind... music is everything... it is all about spiritual contact. She provokes once again: "I am still waiting for you to tell me what you are thinking of doing with your life beyond your doctoral degree." I wonder if this question relates to returning to Brazil, remaining in the USA, or returning to Nigeria? I am not sure how to answer it at the moment. I know that I will take due advantage of the opportunities as they come. The provocations continue: "Are you befriending someone over there? Do I have any justification to be analyzing things as I am doing? Am I being provocative for no reason? Are you eating well and taking care of your health?" These are caring and appreciated questions from a true lover. The answers are not as simple since any answer will still be interrogated. That's just being Lúcia. I can just see her stimulating provocative conversations between us indefinitely.

The core of the communication of mid-March of 1988, dated February 28, after many digressive flows of emotions and love, rests on Lúcia's hope that one day, I might be waiting for her at home instead of my many letters waiting for her. Wishful thinking, again! Love is incredibly innocent and vulnerable. She enumerates those who know about our relationship: from immediate family members to colleagues at work. I must have asked that silly question in a previous communication. She highlights a number of events of her life such as taking classes in English, swimming, and taking Yoga classes. In the midst of all these activities, she laments my painful absence. She invokes a series of desires: "Every day, my desires are heightened. The desire to see you, feel your shoulders wrapping my body, feel your body in mine, see your shining eyes in mine, your eyes are like small traffic lights that keep changing. Your eyes are

3 - Mixed re-encounters

bright and expressive… When am I going to receive your body in mine…? When am I going to feel you without uttering a single word…?"

Yes, this is the crux of the matter. The defining essence of this cosmic perambulation is simply this: distance, a lack of physicality, a lack of tangible warmth. It is the ephemerality of emotions and the persistence of elusive love. Lúcia sees herself in the midst of a multitude of faces, decisions, wishes, power, objectives to achieve, and the obstacles inhibiting those goals. As I relive these aspirations, it dawns on me that these spontaneities are distressing and therapeutic all at the same time. Their intensity scares my soul to its fragile bones. For how long will two lovers continue to have these elusive dreams? I would not know. But of one thing I am sure, we complete each other despite the unbearable distance. I would not give anything up at this point. Painful, yes, but hopefully not for a very long time before everything returns to normalcy. Why not?

The saga of Lúcia continued for a long time, even longer than one can possibly imagine. The love affair in Salvador that led to the birth of Bidemi before my exit to the USA was to come back to haunt me. A few years after completing my Master's degree, I felt the need to reunite with Bidemi. I had even made arrangements to get him admitted in a local school in Wisconsin. To my surprise, the American Embassy in Rio de Janeiro denied his immigration visa as a student. Rather, I was advised by the Embassy to apply for him as a permanent resident since he was my child. That was not to happen for another few years after I had completed the doctorate degree and gotten a job to sponsor him. I was back in Brazil to try to get Bidemi a visa after securing a professional position, and on both trips, I stopped by São Paulo to see Lúcia and her family. There were mixed feelings upon seeing her new life. She has added two more children over the years. That did not affect our feelings. I felt comfortable with the three kids and played the role of a father for a very short time. Once the American visa issue was resolved for Bidemi, he was settled in the USA and assimilated the American culture quickly. Though I maintained close contacts with Lúcia, new professional challenges would hinder constant visits and soon, I realized that I had to focus on overcoming the odds to stabilize myself professionally. It was in the course of these career developments and limited visit to São Paulo that I learned of the demise of Lúcia. Oh, what a shocking pain! The August Flower was no more.

Sandro and Fayola.
©Barbosa Archives 2018

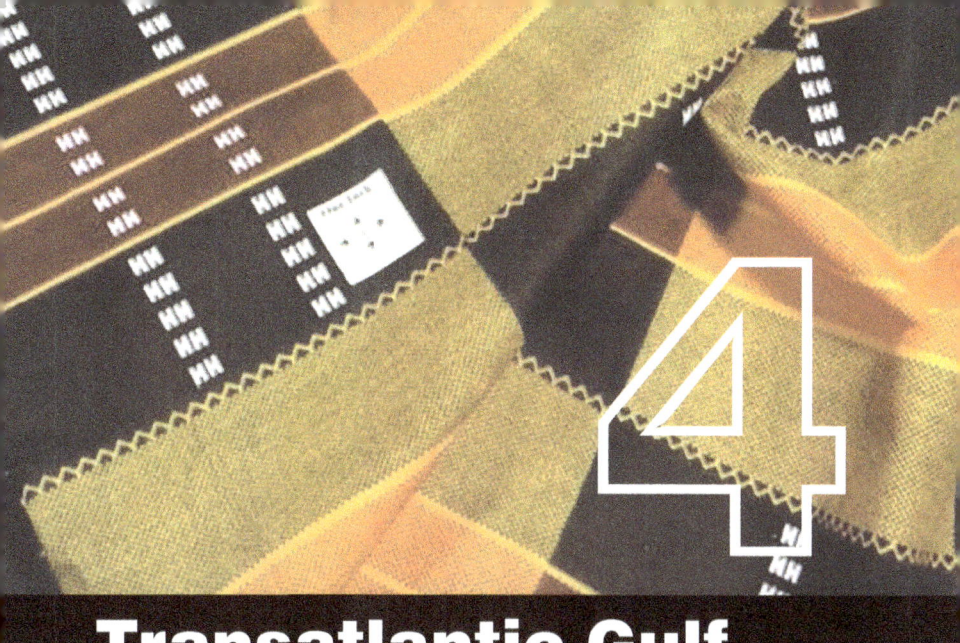

4

Transatlantic Gulf

Vera Barbosa
©Barbosa Archives 1995

Separation between lovers is like inducing the aroma of death. Nostalgia is the mother of such a macabre aroma in the sense that all that is left to console the fragmented spirit are the relics of space, place, and memories in general. It is similar to that moment at the train station or the airport, where lovers are holding hands, embracing, passionately kissing, and unable to let go. As the last boarding announcements are made, they would look each other in the face, while asking the rhetorical question: "How soon shall we see each other again? Are we going to be alright while waiting to see each other all over again?" The aroma reeks of death because though both lovers are alive, they are not physically present with each other to be able to ascertain that aliveness. The distance digs a huge gulf between lovers. Consequently, separation steals the aroma of life and replaces it with that of pain. Anguish due to a series of departures, coupled with the uncertainty of reencounter, becomes the order of the day.

Even after the necessary separation, memories and homesickness conspire to maintain some level of sanity with the painful passage of time. I knew that our love was real even if it did require a great deal of my time and other unquantifiable sacrifices. Sustaining the hope of reunion someday served as the only motivation to hold on to the relationship from a remote location. Worse still, voluntary separation from Africa and Brazil in the quest for a better life in the United States included lofty dreams and tales of trauma that the subconscious struggled to keep under control. I remember it well; the date was August 20. Lúcia was still in São Paulo. I was in Brasília. We had gradually lost contact because her communication after my unceremonious departure from São Paulo to Salvador had been less frequent. Could the transatlantic gulf be the catalyst to a rekindling of our passionate love? Atlantic separation was a double-edged sword: the invisible pain and the visible effort to soothe the pain through the intensity of cosmic messages. My departure from Brazil en route to the USA was a different experience than leaving Nigeria for Brazil. Though the hope to stay on in Brazil was dashed, the prospects of a new beginning in the United States gave me such a high level of fulfillment. It was as if the separation created a new path to success. When I look back today at the sacrifices and uncertainties during that time, it feels good that it was not all in vain. On some level, I wish Lúcia was still alive to see the aftermath of her contribution linger on. Atlantic separation was more desirable than the dose of death that took her away from her loved ones, including from her graceful children. Occasionally, on her mom's birthday, I read Fayola's Facebook post reminiscing about her singular mother-angel: "Though you are not physically here with me, your love keeps me going and I strive to make you proud for all the beautiful things you taught me. I will never be able to forget you because for me you are all I have and I feel you live inside of me. Happy birthday!" This is a more painful separation. Atlantic separation carries echoes of lives submerged in the ocean, lives permanently marooned under the sea, and lives that may never be recuperated except through spiritual invocations. Atlantic separation has robbed me twice. My ancestors were forcibly removed from Africa, and now here I am taking a different (and voluntary) journey. I am being separated from Africa and Brazil—two locations implicated in the Atlantic slavery as well as these narratives of memorialization.

En route to the USA, an experience in Chicago made me feel oppressed. Racism gave some people the reckless power to dominate others: It all dates back to slavery. Otherwise, how else could a young white girl feel she had the right to provoke the only black man on the plane? How could a biased white community side with the white girl and get away with it despite the facts and circumstances? I am not sure they got away with it as I chose not to pursue the injustice. I had better things to focus on. I was also new in the country and did not know any better in terms of pursuing justice to the bitter end, and how it could have affected my studies. Was it worth giving up on my dreams? The black man is always the guilty one before and after the fact. Why waste my precious time? I would not know if it was the best decision I made to simply let it go. Rationally speaking, I felt it was the best decision since I won the case. Despite winning in the court of law, I told my Attorney it was not worth my time to pursue civil damages against the state of Illinois and divine justice was swifter. I was content with winning symbolically, but I also felt I really did not win. A negative stigma had been created around me. I was the only African on a local American flight that got harassed and arrested. Even on the inside, the stigma permanently disrupts my composure each time I feel psychologically attacked and racially profiled. It is an episode I have never been able to forget. Somehow, I was unable to dwell on it in my correspondence with Lúcia as she would have been burdened, scared, and upset. She would probably have encouraged me to return to Brazil immediately. That would even have been a risk. What investment did I have in Brazil to warrant any such peace of mind? None. There was no way to calculate how she would eventually cope with the fact that I was back in her arms again—begging for love and affection like a spoiled baby. There was no saying how she would react. I could not fathom the possibility of a second rejection, given the circumstances. Not achieving one's dream in Brazil was pardonable, but failing at the American dream was not! It would have been read as a perpetual failure. Regardless of my motivations to confront my challenges and make the best of life in the USA, Atlantic separation was indeed a catalyst to my newly found energy and vitality. I could not possibly have taken it for granted. I felt privileged. I needed to succeed.

The incessant energy that separation engenders often propels a certain continuity of desires and aspirations that may be elusive on the surface, but do have their therapeutic function. In one of her correspondence, Lúcia estimates that in her assessment of 120 days, I had written 57 letters to her that amounted to 130 pages in total. On average, that is like writing a letter per day. Where does such energy come from? I often wonder if it is a unique opportunity to document a precious life, a loved one, and a phenomenal personality. It was separation in both life and death because even while she was alive, the relationship was mostly of a distant nature. The effort to keep it alive only took place in the imagination. Wherever she is, to embrace a human being full of wisdom, affection, and love is a delight. I behold a human being who surpasses description. As I navigate her words all over again and creatively read them in consonance with mine, I realize people come into our lives for a reason. We may appreciate them, we may value them, we may overanalyze them, but what is important is that when compared to others who have passed through us, they represent this enchanting enigma of a being made for posterity as well as a being engaged with us in order to uniquely impact our lives. Very few people occupy such a powerful place of memory in our lives.

    When life takes its twists and turns, we fail to see the positives in life's lessons because while going through the pain of the moment, we hardly see a purpose. As I compose this memory, I am sitting in an airport and I see the anxiety in the faces of stranded travelers. Their bodies are moving past each other with a sense of urgency to get to their destinations. The question on everyone's mind is the expectation that this technological bird gets everyone home. Yet, my eyes remain fixed on this narrative of the soul. Lúcia is everywhere, yet nowhere. Her presence is all I need to summon the energy to keep going even as I engage what I see as a narrative of perdition and hope. As usual, in some quick notes appended to an accompanying correspondence, she alludes to the joy of meeting someone who completes her, someone who talks about the heart, affection, and concerns for humanity in this ephemeral world. She even invokes solitude to become her friend. It is indeed an irony to invite a negative vibe to be a friend in the sense of a negation of a negation while communicating a melancholic feeling. With fall lectures ending in December and spring ones starting in January, the communication covers the end of my first semester and the beginning of the new one. It is a Twilight Zone of stress, anxiety, and a feeling of growth despite bitter experiences and continuous culture shock.

The opening was quite emotionally explosive: "Sweet Love, you really want to know? I love you!!!" This is powerful. It conveys an intense feeling that only the lover can put in such poetic language. What follows is a mix of context and conspiracy of change in terms of my complaints about loneliness. She referenced my phone call that gave her joy but played the role of the therapist when she insisted on my seeing the positive side of my current solitude. She recognized that it was easy for her to simply expect me to be super human. At the same time, she recognized the full extent of pain that loneliness engenders for many. She acknowledged that after we ended our phone calls, she felt like embracing me and getting on a plane to be with me that very moment. While she gave the date of her vacation as the week of July 18 and after, she also tried to make me see the reality that I was not in the worst predicament in life:

> "My love, think about the positive side of your loneliness. You are healthy, aren't you? Think about it. There are many people in the hospital, some with no arms nor legs. Many negative things are happening all around us. People are exterminating an entire family. I read some newspapers this week talking about shootings in California, at the University of Texas in Austin, at McDonalds, etc. So, my beloved, let us think that in the midst of broader ills going on in the world, your dilemma is minuscule."

This is a powerful reality check that I needed for my own psychological balance. She philosophizes that I see loneliness as a friend and not as an enemy in order to overcome its power over me. She uses her own life as an example by stating that at times she wants to be left alone. She concludes that nothing is negative about loneliness. It is only a matter of time for the stress to dissipate. While I am refuting and battling loneliness, she herself desires moments of loneliness as a source of power to reflect. She adds, "It is a paradox!"

As Lúcia responds to my previous communication, she acknowledges that she was not dating anyone in Brazil and her life revolved around me. She commented on her photo of 1982 in comparison to that of 1987 in which she was five years older. She felt playfully like a witch, for good or for ill, all for Clétus. She also wondered if she was the person I wanted in my life. She philosophizes that once human beings find themselves in a new situation, they become conflicted. She recognized that given my sensibility in calling her a poet based on her writings, she felt re-assured. She shared some prophecies by some Afro-Brazilian spiritual leaders who suggested that 1988 will be a difficult year as an illness worse than AIDS will emerge. Relationships will be threatened and arguments will be rampant among lovers. Worse still, as I proceeded in understanding Lúcia's analysis, there emerged a new line of thought about confusion and wishful thinking. Lúcia proposes two possibilities: The first is to rush my doctoral program and complete it in less time and the second is to figure out collectively how we can be together. The first comes with a high level of ambivalence and risk. On the one hand, Lúcia was communicating a possible solution to my loneliness by completing the program hurriedly; a proposal that is irrational and almost impossible. A doctoral program cannot be completed in two years. On the other hand, she was trying to push the responsibility of decision making on me which makes sense but also creates a sense in which I had to consider the alternative of actually abandoning the program. The thought of this possibility is indeed contradictory since she recently emboldened me to see loneliness as a friend and not let it be an excuse to give up on the program. This situation, while not impacting my decision to continue with the program, created an urgency and confusion all at the same time. Lúcia recently expressed strength in solidarity with my goals, she also appreciated her feeling so useful and supportive of me which gave her life some special meaning; but soon, she is weakened by her own desires and flesh. She states: "I am unable to write anything else with eloquence, the only sentiment that overwhelms my soul, is the desire to be with you. Tell me, my beloved, what can I do to cope with this heartfelt desire?" Without any answer from my end, with so much going through my own head about a woman who is suffering in love because of me, she lamented the fate of pretenders she had turned down who wondered why she could possibly be preserving herself for someone who is so far away. It is a sign of depression. Within a frame of three months that took her to respond to a series of communication in one poignant reflective analysis, she has moved from total support of a lover to a sense of self-preservation and nervous breakdown. Is this the beginning of distancing or the emergence of clarity? My soul seeks resolution.

In the endless game of supportive and reality-check communications from Lúcia, I get somewhat confused about how to deal with the shifting feelings of hope and disappointment. Lúcia often wears many caps—a lover, an encourager, a spiritual guide, a realist, and a provocateur. Her latest communication was indeed a provocation. Her goal to be passionate yet frank with me in terms of what I needed to face in order to be successful at my professional objective was a mixed message. She went to the extreme end of things as she insisted that self-reflection was a normal process of life. As she responded to my issues from a previous communication, she also came to terms with her own challenges by stating almost convincingly: "I know something for sure. I no longer want to suffer. This is one of the reasons I raise issues with you concerning what you really want; and you get upset or irritated. I hope you do not feel that I am using your words against you." Beyond her own reflections about failed relationships and disappointments in life, what strikes me most is the way Lúcia made a counter move when it comes to my complaints about my experiences with a new American system. She was candid in stating that I needed to face the reality of challenges that come with professional development. Graduate school is not a place for toddlers. It is a place of self-extension that leads to growth. She describes the growing pains in the context of "thorns of the profession." Every profession has its pain and sacrifice. If it means reading and reading more, analyzing and analyzing more, producing and producing more, then that is the price to pay for success. Yet, if I felt the pressure was too much, I could consider giving it all up with future regrets. She states: "You chose this path, did you not? If you want it, this is what it takes; if not, hit the road, Jack. There are millions and millions of people wanting to be in your shoes. Even whites are struggling to be in such a privileged position. Imagine black people, huh?" As usual, she tries to joke about the weather, teasing me about the cold and how I must be suffering and needing warmth. In her own style, she was on the one hand inviting me to come to Brazil for warmth, and at the same time she was encouraging me to face my reality of sacrifice by focusing on my studies.

A follow up phone call from Lúcia complained of my lack of cosmic communication, but it was not deliberate on my part. It was more of the reality of a new semester requiring focus and planning. Her note had expressed sadness for not receiving my letters. The phone did not clarify much just an expression later that she felt I was sad. With two lovers saddened by distance and homesickness, the solution lies in supporting each other through any form of solace. For Lúcia, it was through letters, phone calls, and honesty. The recent note was actually pleading for me to not stop writing. We shall see the extent to which

I am able to sustain the writing craze. Much of this dialogue took place over a period of a year. There were follow-ups only after my life stabilized in the USA, but the idea then was not to reconnect with Brazil or Lúcia but to make sense of my new life. I often wonder if the period was locked in space, time, and purpose as if once that dream of being together was realized as impossible, the communication stopped. Yet, the communication was so intense that it could not be forgotten easily. Was its effect a kind of therapy for a traumatic phase of life? Were the memories of the past connected with symptoms of intrusion that go back in time to evaluate these memories? According to psychologists, intrusive memories include (1) Recurrent and distressing memories of the traumatic event; (2) Reliving the event through flashbacks; (3) Nightmares about the traumatic event; and (4) Severe emotional distress. As traumatic as being delayed in life is, being stigmatized and discriminated against and feeling a sense of injustice all over again, it's as if my success is minimalized. These memories may be intrusive only when the negative sides are recollected. They can also be emboldening and encouraging when positive outcomes are remembered. What led to wanting to remember the events were actually triggered by not wanting to forget the role Lúcia played in that vital year of assimilation in the USA that was filled with confusion and paranoia. Regardless of the pain and sacrifice, the ultimate outcome is fulfilling. In looking back in order to look forward, I arrived at some preliminary conclusions about the experiences. When we do not allow the contours of life to stop us, we eventually overcome the odds and succeed. We must celebrate those who stepped in with us to face the battle of life such as Lúcia and many others like her who played the role of God to get us through hardships of life. When we honestly celebrate such contributors to our success in life, we are also opening new doors for more blessings in our lives.

There is definitely a therapeutic function to the transatlantic communication: The expectation of the letters, the waiting, the anguish when they do not come, and the certainty that the effect would be calming and transformative. This helped the process of healing even while the experience was still going on. On both sides, there was anxiety, especially anxiety about the future. For me, it was about completing my degree in the midst of culture shock and normalized racism. For her, it was about the possibility of fulfilling the dreams of getting together as a couple. The latter was not to happen. Yet, I credit her for her role in encouraging me in the course of my travails. A spiritual dimension seems to have overwhelmed the entire experience. I got wiser and more spiritual. Two biblical stories come to mind when it comes to the spirituality of my experience. I can relate to Joseph who was sold into slavery by his brothers and to David who recovered all after being besieged by war and losing to his enemies. Both stories are comforting to the soul. Ultimately, victory is manifested and the once oppressed emerges as victorious. In the case of Joseph, he spent 13 years in prison, from the time he was sold into captivity by his envious brothers, to the time he was promoted to the second highest position in Egypt. Joseph did not rise to power easily, however. He took over from Potifar's cupbearer within two years. The remaining years, he was either serving Potifar or in prison. On account of Joseph's faithfulness, he found favor with Pharaoh who saw that God's hands were with him. Pharaoh entrusted him with all he had and Potifar prospered on account of Joseph. As Joseph rose in power, so did the interest in him by Potifar's wife. She made persistent advances to Joseph to sleep with her but failed. Though Joseph resisted many times, Potifar's wife eventually grabbed his garment while Joseph ran away from her. The garment became the evidence she needed to use against him by denouncing him to Potifar. The husband accused Joseph of rape: "The Hebrew slave, whom you brought to us, came in to me to make sport of me; and it happened as I raised my voice and screamed, that he left his garment beside me and fled outside" (Genesis 39: 13-18). Joseph continually prayed to God to save him from this evil woman. God answered his prayers by keeping him in jail, an unpleasant location to gain political experience and governance. Joseph suffered in order to rise to power. Joseph's spiritual gift to interpret dreams came in handy when Pharaoh needed someone to interpret his dreams. His resistance to Potifar's wife was a test of character. While the purpose of our suffering may not be initially clear; in the end, when all things work together for our good, we realize God's hands even in our suffering. It is against this biblical background that I see a parallel in my experience and that of Joseph.

The other character that gives me consolation as I contemplate my own experiences of loss, delay, restoration, and success, emerges in the figure of David, who lost and recovered all. While away from their land, the Amalekites came to take their children and wives captive and burned down Ziklag. The experience made Israelites sad and they wept incessantly. They were so distressed that they thought of stoning David to death. David inquired of the Lord what to do. The Lord instructed him to pursue and overtake. Some of David's men were too weak to cross the river and they had to continue without them. Along the way, they met a weak Egyptian, and they gave him food and drink. As the weak man regained strength, they asked him who he was and he explained that he was the servant of one of the Amalekite raiders. He had become sick and the master left him for dead. He begged David to spare his life in exchange for showing the location of the raiders. David agreed. When David and his men saw the raiders, they were having a big celebration. David attacked and killed most of them, though about 400 fled. David swiftly recovered everything he had lost—all the wives and children—including new flocks and herds. David even decided to give spoils to the 200 men who were too weak to continue the fight. This shows the astuteness of David as warrior and king. Both Joseph and David offer strength and hope in the midst of painful events. The memories would not have had this impactful effect if not for the depth of the events. Separation is like mourning. A departure of a loved one who may well be going on a journey of return or no return. There was no way to predict the return and victory. All that could be speculated is the courage necessary to face life. Lúcia stood guard protecting the fortress of mind and space, hoping that one day this separation would become history and a celebration of victory. Though victory came about, it was in stages. The Joseph-David figure who recovered all did not return to share the glories of victory. Instead, he chose to continue the path of life as struggle after struggle overwhelmed his life. Even today as I write, critical distance was necessary to absorb the stress. I am in no condition to liken myself to Joseph or David but their experiences of grief do resonate with the feeling of being deprived of family, status, and meaning of life, only to be recuperated many decades after. In this sense, it was worth celebrating the symbolic victory even after the fact. Lúcia may not be alive to share in this celebration but her presence is felt in the messages that I hear from her and through my pen as she helps to write. After all, the memories are not all mine. They are our memories.

    Many are the days of distress when abnormality is the order of the day. The separation, while painful, was a period of transformation as the soul aspires to a better life. A typical day in Brasília was a constant series of distress. Scholarship was not in sight. Feeding was dependent on a good-willed Emmanuel, and the rest of the balancing act of schooling was just a matter of chance. Without basic financial resources, focus was impossible. Sexual encounters and occasional drunkenness became a routine goal of expiation that takes the mind off deprivation. Breakfast was nil. Satisfaction of hunger was based solely on the Cafeteria lunch. It was all the body needed to reinvigorate itself on a daily basis. Luckily, classes were in the late afternoon for graduate students. Once the urging of the body was satisfied, it was easy to focus on study at the library. The mind often wonders at the library: amidst the dream of success, lack of funds, and distraction from daily issues of struggle and frustration. Hope held it all together, for without hope everything is lost. On some rare occasions, I get so overwhelmed that I miss class for not having completed the readings for the day. Hunger and study are not congenial twins. The following week, I will run into classmates who would not only provide synthesis of the classes I missed but gestured how they covered my absence in class. I often appreciated the gesture even if disappointed at myself for allowing depression to overtake my goals. Emmanuel did not know of such moments as he must have felt he was doing his best to help. Presentations were my best. I enjoyed them—it was an opportunity to perform, to prove myself, and to give it my all. On such occasions, I felt good about myself. I even managed to register for seminars such as one on linguistic dialectology and another on "crimes of passion" that was based on Clarice Lispector. I was able to follow the seminar and presentations by many established presenters. I do not recall their names now, but I learned a lot. I had not heard much of Clarice Lispector. Given the nature of the absurdity that ran through the lives and actions of the short stories protagonists, I saw myself in some of them and was consoled that I was not alone after all. I was able to locate myself in some of the claricean characters. My situation was not as extreme as Macabéia who succumbed to death at the moment of success as in *The Hour of the Star*. The characters of *Family Ties* are no less problematic. Their epiphanic moments reveal intense agony and the search for closure. The "Birthday" was one such story when the mother felt unloved and neglected. Despite the presence of her children on her anniversary, their actions towards her made her realize her own estrangement and detachment. Though I did not feel all the love I could have had, I had enough to get me through the tough times. That was enough consolation for me.

Living in Brazil was not only academic for me. It was an opportunity to assimilate aspects of a culture that I have come to value over the years. At the same time, the socio-economic conditions that affect local people often affect the foreigner in a more egregious manner. One is then compelled to follow the events as if trying to stay afloat amid all of the constraints. The 1980s were years of concern in both Brazil and Nigeria. I often wonder if I would have left Nigeria if the conditions were more conducive to professional development and educational attainment. The reality is that either way, for someone needing a higher degree in a rare field, I had to travel from home. Brazil was the only option available since I had been there before and loved it. The 1980s in Brazil was a period marred by a cycle of economic and social crises that remained unending. Issues of social conflicts and upheavals that date back to the violence of the colonial past play out in social protests and resistance.

Despite numerous acts of protest over the years, Brazilians have managed to be a peaceful people. This sounds like a contradiction of terms since Brazil has passed through tough transitions to democracy and modernization without any violent change. Even the end of colonial rule was a simple declaration of independence without bloodshed. This is not to undermine the brutal extermination of the Amerindian population and the violence of slavery against Africans who were forcibly removed from their motherland. Beyond these examples, most of the major Brazilian conflicts were resolved through nonviolent means. Regional or local conflicts such as the Cabanagem (1835), the War of the Farrapos (1845), and the São Paulo Civil War (1932) were resolved peacefully. The *canudos* resistance described in Euclides da Cunha's *Os sertões* (translated as *Rebellion in the Backlands*) was relatively peaceful. Yet, on a daily basis, violence was the norm. Whether it was the rural bandits of the Northeast who fought rival bandits and backlands colonels in the 1900s, the rural workers fighting the landowners as exemplified by the famous Chico Mendes (leader of the rubber-tappers), a rubber-tapper killed in Acre in 1988; or the corrupt police officers who were themselves part of criminal activities such as in the *favelas* (ghettos) of Rio de Janeiro: it is obvious that Brazil has endured a pattern of contemporary violence.

By the time of the military dictatorship (1964-1985), violence had been moderated as a corporatist gesture by making some concessions to workers and thereby avoiding direct class confrontation against the privileged. Though the military regime deployed torture and mass killings that led to exile of some patriots, democratic pressures gained the upper hand that led to a more popular political participation. Somehow, despite repression, explosive revolution was avoided. However, by the late 1970s and early 1980s, a number of social movements sprang up fueled by the middle class, workers, and women, to challenge the powerful elite. Some of these movements morphed into NGOs with financial support or donations from abroad. With the rise of economic crisis, hunger, and misery into the 1990s, the government introduced compensatory social policies that improved social services and quality of life for the masses. Despite introduction of some social services, the masses still felt marginalized and excluded, while social mobility remained stagnant. Economic policies steered towards social stabilization unfortunately led to structural unemployment and slower economic growth. It is clear that economic growth, redemocratization processes, and government social benefits alone will not solve the problem. While inequality persists, there is ample evidence that more political participation is affecting social change towards better equity in Brazil.

Beyond these social contexts, the thoughts of Lúcia are at the core of the soothing of the frame of mind that haunts the soul. As it rains on the Jamaican audience during the all-star tribute to Bob Marley, entitled *One Love*, I am inspired by the song, "No Woman, No Cry," sung by Jimmy Cliff. As I continue to listen to the gyrating melody and the lyrics, the memory of Lúcia comes alive: "No woman no cry / …I remember when we used to sit / In the government yard in Trenchtown / Oba, observing the hypocrites /As they would mingle with the good people we meet / Good friends we have had, oh good friends we've lost along the way (way) / In this bright future you can't forget your past / So dry your tears I say" (Bob Marley). It is not as if she has any reason to cry despite having gone to the beyond without the benefits of the seeds she left behind. What makes Bob Marley's song resonate lies in the nostalgia of her presence. Loving, kind, affable, and good-willed: Lúcia gave me an opportunity to feel loved. She is the epitome of the complete human being. Listening to the melody of Marley brings memories. I remember the days of going to the park, days of eating at the Cafeteria or at restaurants in São Paulo, going to the movie theater to see a historical movie, mingling with Afro-Brazilian writers and critics she was familiar with and loved, visiting the Butantã Institute, the statue of the Bandeirantes, and just goofing around town like new lovers without any inhibition. Those were great times without any precise qualification. Those were special days of taking me home to meet the family, of sharing her family with me as if I was the only person left for her in this world to love… I could not but feel privileged because she was a genuine soul. My career may have taken a new turn. I probably would not have been so impacted by Brazil if not for falling in love with her at first sight. I drew strength and continue to draw strength from her wealth of love.

Despite my adventurous experiences in São Paulo and Salvador, my days in Brasília were numbered. In the midst of the cataclysmic perambulations of life, I was focused yet confused. Classes were a means of escaping boredom and affliction of uncertainty. They were also an ample indication that there was a long journey ahead to fulfillment. In the back of my mind, though the afflictions may last a night, there was joy in the morning. I recall the good spirits of Brazilian students in the long-stretched architectural *Minhocão*, international students and roommates living in the *Centro Olímpico*, and mingling all across campus. In their supportive eyes and demeanor, I felt a sense of joy that I was closer to my destiny than ever before. Unfortunately, the funds were not immediately available. The distance from home gave a lasting sense of nostalgia. The Lúcias of life were few and far-between. Other than very few friends of Emmanuel who also invited me out, I did not have my own circle of friends. I could not even afford to take them out. It was such a dependent condition. In retrospect, one must be grateful to God for even bringing me to the fulfilling point I am today. It is part of the mystery of life that the uncertainties of life have been majorly transformed. The journey was combative and full of risks. The different agents of hindrance have been put to shame. Yet the memories of that long journey refuse to be truncated. The adventures of Salvador were also to come to haunt me. I found out through a phone call that the mother of a child I left behind had visited me in Nazaré looking for presence and support. It was not to be. Though I did the bare minimum of visiting the family in Salvador to express joy and support, it took me only about a month to get the necessary papers and visa to leave for the USA. Of course, the preparations had been ongoing. The incidents were pre-destined and pre-ordained. I would not know how else to see things in such an impossible moment. They were of course about reaching for a better life. Within less than six months in Brasília, my luck changed dramatically. I attended classes for less than three months because I gained admission to five American universities and was making a decision about which one to attend. I faced obstacles with people that I expected would support my dreams… I was disappointed. In the end, the House of the Lord came to the rescue. Departure from Brazil was a miracle. The hibernating moments were preparatory. The success ahead was inevitable. It was a divine design and I was just the vehicle of fulfillment.

Though I had never been to the United States at the time, while in Brazil, the visit of President Reagan to Brazil in 1986 gave me some insights into Brazilian-American relations. A dream of America has always been at heart but so unreal. One never knows when history is being made. Unbeknownst to me, leaving Nigeria in the first place was the beginning of that possible dream. Even for my graduate program, I was flexible though Brazil remained the first choice. America was filled with opportunities and possibilities. Yet, for about a year of loafing and searching in Brazil, it was not clear whether the USA was going to have such an impact on my professional development. Life is full of mysteries that defy the mind. I had contemplated going to the USA as early as 1980 after completing high school. I had an opportunity to visit France and had a brother in Illinois. I contacted him from France that I was interested in coming to the USA. Though the efforts proved abortive, I appreciate them as it gave me an insight about the difficulty in obtaining an American visa. That visit could also have changed my destiny. In retrospect, I appreciate waiting until I was more mature in order to be better adjusted to the American system. As two reluctant global partners, USA and Brazil have had a somewhat rocky relationship. It was difficult to define common priorities while one was against nuclear know how and debt forgiveness while the other expected an active position in the global Cold War. The result was a mismatch of priorities on both sides throughout the 1980s. Both countries could not agree on free and fair trade as tariffs were imposed on both partners—causing long-term trade tensions. The USA eventually recognized Brazil as an emerging world power that needed equal partnership. Realizing it could not deter Brazil from reaching out to other countries for support of its nuclear dream and trajectory, the USA capitalized on the debt burden of Brazil to negotiate a gradual dismantlement of the nuclear project which was officially terminated in 1998.

As much as Brazilian-American relations have improved in the 1990s and beyond, it would have been great times to see Lúcia again. Yet, despite professionalization, the time was never right to give back what this angel has given to me in immeasurable sacrifices. I had gotten married and had pressures on the family front. Unfortunately, she gave up the ghost in 2004. All I have left beyond my own memories being recollected is a short story she also wrote four years earlier. For a therapist who circulates amidst writers but fails to see herself as a writer, it was a delight to open an anthology and find her therein. It brought back memories. Entitled "August Flower... Happiness," it struck a mixed chord of affection and nostalgia. It was like reliving some memories all over again. Lúcia opens the story with the moment of encounter in the Circular Bus and ends with a note the character, Clétus, had left for her:

> *You brought me vigorous happiness. You exuded honesty, love, affection,*
> *and unconditional dedication, which helped me to tap the felicity that has*
> *always been within me. From this day onward, I live and will live serenely*

> *searching my horizons, transforming that we have grown. I don't know how*
> *to explain how you transmitted all this to me, but this is how I feel since I*
> *met you. With deep feelings, and wishing you felicity as well.*
> *Clétus.*

The story itself captured moments of love, passion, hope, anxieties about the future, and the painful reality of separation when Clétus left for the USA. Despite the painstaking efforts to fictionalize the relationship within a short story, all I could imagine is Lúcia being alive. Though this is a fantasy, the precious story remains a vital material memory that can console my soul. She may have gone to join the ancestors, but through this aesthetic transformation, the soul and mind are indeed revitalized. I remain indebted to her love. I remain redeemed by this transatlantic separation turned memories.

Cosmic Whispers

Vera Barbosa
©Barbosa Archives 1995

5
The American Journey

Niyi Afolabi
©Afolabi Archives 2010

Even before my arrival in Brasília to pursue graduate studies, the prospect of leaving for the United States or Europe was already in motion. I was pursuing admission with at least a half a dozen universities spread across three continents: Latin America, the United Sates, and Europe. It was just a matter of when and where. I was clear in my vision of attaining the doctorate. I had left Nigeria with a feeling of frustration that I could not pursue a graduate program in Portuguese in that same system where I had been hired to start a degree program. It was an honorable position that also carried a risk. The risk of wasting away with no one to mentor or provide me with the skills needed to be secure and functional. I needed professional growth and development. In the wish for a professional life, I had contacted many experts I knew through learned journals to give me a sense of direction. A few responded with enthusiasm. Some also shared the frank realities of the field. Despite the mixed responses, I was determined to pursue my dreams. I was not sure what I was doing but I knew I had to do something to get out of the stagnation of an academic environment where all people did was settle for mediocrity.

In those times and climes, survival was the word of the day. I was the proverbial "star" of the moment in terms of youthful age and I was determined to move that prospect into the next level. The next level was traveling abroad. The stakes were quite high. I had lost my dad right after completing my undergraduate degree. My mom was doing fine but struggling financially. My sisters were not as academically prepared to take care of themselves. I was at a privileged crossroads moment of sadness and joy. I could not afford to lose that special moment by settling into a lavish life that will only lead to stagnation and dependency by others and on others. I had to make my move and make it quickly. I was ready to "check out" and check out I did! Looking back, it was the smartest decision I ever made. The excuse was to pursue admission letter and return to pursue the funding. The first happened but the latter did not. It was complicated. It meant persuading my employer to sponsor my graduate program for the next five years with the assurance that I would be returning to Nigeria. My only illusion was that I did not even know when I would be returning. It was a kind of obvious dead-end. In the end, I resolved to stay on in Brazil to pursue my dreams and risk it all—that is, the prospect of losing the very dream job that could have stabilized the family. I wanted more. I could afford the risk. I was young and dynamic. I needed to explore the possibilities life had to offer me despite the odds.

Once in Brasília, the challenges came in crescendo but were not a match for the solutions divine providence had prepared for me. One regret, perhaps more of a persistent question on my mind, was if things could have been different with Lúcia being permanently in my life all this while. She surely did her part. She sacrificed in her own way. Nonetheless, all I am left with were memories of our correspondence. A particular one summed up in a chronological manner our communications over six months. This indicates a personal passion to document the cosmic communication that was quite unique. The first was from Orlando in which I had provided a Wisconsin address to maintain communication. The second, now after arrival in Wisconsin, shared moments of transition such as finding an apartment and settling down to the new academic year. I had also wondered if she were doing fine as knowing she would be my only consolation since I was so lonely. The third was a mix of three postcards that indicated that I was at peace for receiving news from Lúcia, now that classes had started. The fourth was the very first letter that touched on the issue of the Chicago unfortunate scar, a part of which reads: "Lúcia, I confess that what bothers me the most was that incident of racial injustice in Chicago. I have already related everything to you in coded form, but I keep reflecting on it as it was a complete absurdity." While this episode continues to be abbreviated due to the memory of pain it engenders, I am hoping that I could narrate it in detail in some other future context. The fifth letter responded to Lúcia's sadness at my departure and promised to write poems as a coping strategy. She enumerated the poems as they capture the shifting moods of the writer: "If I return"; "If I remain"; If I remain alive"; and "If I die." Such are the complexities of the frame of mind that betrays a soul in complete disarray. Somber moments were those indeed. They were better overcome through divine positive thinking.

As Lúcia accompanies the chain of events that were defining my world in a new country, I also started feeling a sense of anguish regarding the aftermath of the Chicago incident. I was preparing to appear in court. What a nightmare in a foreign country! There was a weight of anxieties. I needed to communicate my state of mind to a loved one such as Lúcia. Part of my inner reflections as captured in my communication reads: "Even as I write, I feel some headache, perhaps a cerebral lesion... but not that I am losing my mind." It was obvious that the incident was achingly weighing on my mind and was bothering me intensely. Beyond the anxieties of the Chicago affair, I was becoming very critical of the system that I needed to adjust to as Lúcia captured my observations: "Let the external beauty deceive no one; for what matters most is the internal beauty. The mechanical man is a prisoner of the machine. I know you understand." The next few letters were still focused on Chicago and what happened afterwards. There was a sigh of relief as captured in the eleventh letter: "It is all over! Glory to God! I am writing from Chicago soon after the court proceedings. The young woman did not show up; shame on her, and shame on the system!" Soon after, it felt like I had come back to being myself without the burden of the traumatic incident. I recognized the care and affection emanating from the communication with Lúcia and wondered if that was all I needed. In praising her for the solace I was feeling from across the Atlantic, I invoked the music of Maria Bethânia: "It is so difficult to be without you / It is so sad to be so far away from you / Your love is so delicious."[1] Apparently the love was not just soothing, it was sustaining of life itself. Occasionally, the freedom we had was such that I even wondered in moments when there was silence from her end, what could be going on with her. I even strangely contemplated she was pregnant to justify her silence. I simply provoked the question out of curiosity and sheer estrangement. There was really no reason for the accusation or suspicion; rather, it was a measure to provoke a response from her as she does with me at times. It turned out that there was no cause for alarm. It took almost two weeks for my letters to get to her and about the same time for hers to reach me. It was as if a complete communication took almost a month. This makes the process tedious. I was restless. I wrote more frequently and had to have the patience to get a response. Those were the days of expensive international calls. They were quite brief and rare. There was need for patience and tranquility.

By December of 1987, I had been in the USA for almost six months. The semester was over and the end of the year was already an indication that a new semester was about to begin in the new year of 1988. I made an expensive call to Lúcia as I could not handle the distance and nostalgia any more. It was good for my spirits. We had a quick opportunity to share pleasantries and encourage each other. I also shared my grades that were not as promising as I had envisaged but not as bad given the psychological circumstances I was faced with. That insecure reality put more pressure on me to expend more efforts against the odds. I reflected on the situation of Lúcia. I analyzed how she has combined school, work, and parenting, in order to ensure progress and a balanced life. I consider her a strong woman. She had prophesied that all the hardships I was going through then will soon be in the past and I will soon be famous and forget the obstacles. I had questioned her on when and how all this optimism will come to fruition. I had

---

1   Maria Bethânia, *Gostoso Demais* (São Paulo: Celluloid, 1988).

seriously considered returning to Brazil to escape this feeling of entrapment in the USA given the persistent culture shock. However, there was that side of me that was afraid of failure. I would not want to be seen as someone who gave up due to passing challenges. I knew returning to Brazil by abandoning my studies was all wishful thinking. I did not have the guts to even make that cowardly decision. I had made up my mind to stay until I could claim ultimate victory. In the constant state of loneliness, the music of Maria Bethânia came to the rescue as in the track of "Sonho Meu" (my dream): "My dream / goes looking for someone living afar / my dream / goes to showcase that nostalgia, my dream / with your freedom, my dream / in my sky, the guiding star disappears / the cold dawn only brings me melancholy, my dream…"[2] Though not fully consoled, at least, I felt transported to Brazil and closer to Lúcia. She had inspired me by asking what my typical weekend was like. Well, today is a Saturday; and all I am doing is re-reading her letter and seeking solace in my loneliness. I reflected on all I gave up in Nigeria to travel abroad, especially Brazil: my job, my family, and the peace of mind that came with professional status. Yet, the level of satisfaction was nil since I was just a recent graduate fortunate enough to be trusted with developing a complete degree program in Portuguese. After compiling the letters, I had my breakfast and read and read them, over and over. I knew I had a lot to do with school in terms of accumulated readings and had to start getting ready for final papers. Even then, I did not feel I got much done. It was time to clean up the apartment and my clothes for the week. By the time I realized it, it was already 5 PM. Such was how fast time went by. The August flower is no more. Yet, her letters brought back some emotions: "Nostalgia love, nostalgia, so much nostalgia to see you again, to see the beautiful color of your skin, your

---

[2] Maria Bethânia, "Sonho Meu," Álibi (São Paulo: Universal Music Ltda, 1978).

voice, your words, your smell, feel your body, your sweat… everything went so fast… just so fast… but delicious memories of you remain in my thoughts." I was flattered. It was a mutual feeling. Such strong emotions emanating from loneliness and nostalgia. They could only come from someone who knew one intimately.

The mysterious Chicago affair was taking its mental toll on me as the days and months passed. It was nice to have someone with whom to share my anxieties. I titled the piece "anguish of hope." Lúcia was the only one closest to me at that time. I felt like sharing my state of mind. It was as if through her communication, she was obliging me to lay bare my frame of mind before appearing in Chicago for court proceedings. I was concerned about making her sad by the details and kept things superficial and codified. I was weighing my words as I reflected on my psychological concerns. Even as I wrote then, I was feeling some headache due to the intensity of my thoughts. As much as I was being evasive, I was also revealing so much from the inner mind. It was one o'clock in the morning and the day went by not being able to explain what I did specifically. I was restless for no apparent reason. I went out for a walk to see if I could somehow free myself from these thoughts of fear and entrapment; but I returned without knowing what to do. I drank coffee without milk or sugar, hoping that I would be stimulated enough to study but all to no avail. I could not study. I decided to write to Lúcia. I asked her not to worry. I expressed my sensitivity and need to share my feelings with her. I could not help myself. With so many books to be read, and realizing the cost of tuition and my purpose in the USA, I wondered at the consequences of letting this mental scar affect my academic performance. I was suffering from a mental blockage. I was so scared of the possibility of failure. I realized Lúcia must be wondering if I was the same person at this very crossroads moment of weakness and vulnerability. Was I someone who sacrificed everything to leave his home country, enthusiastic about knowledge, passionate about reading, and yet unable to focus? What could have happened to him? He was lively and vivacious. Now he is so negative and pessimistic. What could have happened to him? I struggled with the reality that I was passing through a moment of anguish. I was not sure what was going on with me. The mental block was so real that I needed to make some connection with that fateful incident fighting my concentration at that moment. Psychologically, that incident affected me so intensely. I was scared. I still could not believe it happened. As the date to show up again in Chicago was approaching, the anxieties increased. It dawned on me that I was going to face a white system and possibly a white judge and wondered if I could ever get justice as a black man in the USA. The white police officers felt they had to protect the white girl who actually caused the entire drama in the plane but I was almost sure that she would not appear. It was just a show. It was set up to distract me from my defined objective in the USA. I was formulating some conspiracy theories in my head for lack of any better explanation for myself. I believe that all that took place was a way of taking advantage of a foreigner. Whatever it was, it had had its impact. The rest was for God to resolve. I was hoping for vindication.

Following my vindication in Chicago, I went to Church the following Sunday to give glory to God. It was nice to see the astonishment of the Judge when he condemned the action of the police officers. It was even more interesting to hear him pronounce the relieving statement: "Chicago does not have any jurisdiction over what transpired in space. The case is dismissed with prejudice. You are free to go." Such quick but puzzling words changed my mindset as I felt an immediate sense of justice. When my Attorney asked me if I wanted to sue the state of Illinois, I told him not to bother since that was not the reason I came to the USA. I was completely relieved that it was all over. The shame here is that of the officers who acted discriminatorily and unprofessionally. No one should have been arrested as the case did not happen in Chicago. It was all a simple and civil misunderstanding that did not warrant any arrest. According to the judge, the officers assumed that I was an African American and it was customary for them to treat African Americans that way in that part of Chicago. I realized it could have been worse and thanked my stars. After it was all over, no one apologized for the treatment—I was just "free to go." What a game! What a shock! I wondered if everyone passing through that court was always "free to go." I should be thanking my stars. Something told me the judge was also sympathetic and reasonable. I was now back to my normal rhythm of life after such a major victory. The mind could be a little deceptive. I tried not to reveal all the details to Lúcia for fear of her getting depressed and worried about me. Now that it was all over, I felt I was editorializing on the events. With so much work pending, so much readings to do, so much projects due for actualization, my excuses are over and must wake up to the reality of stress. The many letters to Lúcia must be controlled and all I could do now is reassure her that all was well. As she had prophesied, I had gracefully overcome the odds.

 The ordeal may be over but it is worth doing a post-event analysis in order to put this event in proper perspective for the reader. "Aggravated assault and battery" as fabricated without any physical contact or weapon involved is not only hyper-exaggerated, but it was a concerted effort to set one up for a trip to prison. As I read the definition of "aggravated assault," I came to terms with the seriousness of the charge. This meant a more serious assault with a deadly weapon even though no weapon was involved. My study also yielded the fact that a person committing such an act must have intended to cause serious bodily injury to another person with a deadly weapon. Yet all that transpired was verbal—simply asking why someone was banging on the tray behind me to cause consistent discomfort such as my inability to sleep was all that I queried. What I found even scarier was the punishment prescribed for such an act: "Aggravated battery as defined in subdivision (e)(1) is a Class X felony. Aggravated battery as defined in subdivision (a)(2) is a Class X felony for which a person shall be sentenced to a term of imprisonment of a minimum of 6 years and a maximum of 45 years."[3] Oh my God! In the first instance, the accusation did not match what transpired. I had been traveling for almost 24 hours and was tired. The trip from Brazil to Miami was long. I tried to get some sleep like every other passenger. There was a young, unaccompanied white girl sitting behind me and she began opening and slamming her tray just for the heck of it. At first I did not make too much of it since I was sitting alone and she was also sitting alone and it was easy for me to change seats within the same aisle, whenever I felt the slamming of tray ad infinitum. Yet, one could only do that for so long especially when trying to get some sleep during a 12-hour trip to Orlando, Florida. The next flight was from Orlando to Chicago. Unfortunately, that was the cursed trip. By the time I realized the oddity of the young girl's acts, it was rather too late. My error perhaps, was not to call the airline hostess to report the incident. Instead, I calmly told the girl to stop slamming the tray repeatedly, but she suddenly started to cry. A fellow passenger reached out to her and got her to his aisle. The next thing I knew was a few police officers approaching me upon arrival in Chicago. Thus began my American lesson in racism. Without any weapon at all, even against the provision of the law, I was falsely accused of a crime. The rest, they say, is history.

In retrospect, the damage done could have been worse. Imagine spending even days in custody, coping with the cost of legal defense, and the ultimate disruption of one's graduate

---

3   https://codes.findlaw.com/il/chapter-720-criminal-offenses/il-st-sect-720-5-12-3-05.html. Accessed July 28, 2018.

program. With the passage of time, it was probably easier to forget or deny the impact on one's psyche. Nonetheless, in reality it is permanent psychological damage. One walks around in total fear of the unknown, constantly wondering if everyone is evil and mean-spirited. Of course, I have met good people in the course of my American journey. In fact, I did meet humane and generous people. I am just wondering if some relics of that experience are still not lingering somewhere in my inner being. Every time I saw injustice, I was quick to judge and blame the system. I was quick to advocate for whomever I saw as the victim. It made sense to me that since innocent people could easily be rail-roaded to jail, so one has to be very careful in what environment one finds oneself for fear of false accusations. Here is a scenario in which a complete naïve foreigner is singled out for negative immersion. I could imagine again the possibility that instead of getting a doctorate degree, spending a considerable amount of time in jail, being crushed by the experience, being sent back to Africa, and never ever recovering from the insanity. One wonders how many Africans have had such an experience in the land of milk and honey. Reflections such as this one permits one to look more critically and self-analytically for what could have been. In all frankness, part of me still lives in fear of such experiences that can easily twist one's destiny. Much of life is fate. Otherwise, how does one explain that near-fiasco on the way into the country in search of greener pastures? It was as if a strange force was pursuing one's every step to conjure up such a deadly fate. I deliberately kept Lúcia out of the loop of the detailed events until I could no longer hold it all inside and needed someone to share the ordeal with. In fragments of jolted spiritual struggle, I creatively unveiled one of the darkest moments of my life. Now in the past, it is an episode that even the strong would find challenging. I wish no such ordeal on anyone.

My unfortunate experience upon entering the USA shattered my American dream to a certain degree. It brought about unforeseen setbacks that could have been avoided. That realization often brings back romantic memories of Brazil as if things were much better there even though it may just have been an illusory sensation. From São Paulo to Salvador and Brasília, the second time I came to Brazil was different. Unlike my first visit when I was sponsored as an exchange student, the second coming was full of risk-taking and chances. I had no funding and was living on faith. Such a condition called for hope in the midst of hardship— I had spent well over a year in Brazil without any steady income. The generosity of Brazilians was to be commended for according me the opportunity to be a scholar. Yet, I gave it all up for the American dream. Good-willed Africans were also to be appreciated for sheltering me when I had nothing. Brasília was such a lonely place in its character as an artificial "new capital" constructed in 1960, and it signaled a sense of alienation for many. Of course, those internal migrants looking for a better life or the foreign workers at the over 100 embassies do not feel the same way. For those who had the funding, working, or the wherewithal, the perspective was more positive. I struggled through the first few months of studying in Brasília while hoping for a better life. The classes were stimulating and engaging, and the professors were equally encouraging. The student body was quite dynamic, too, but for some reason I was always dreaming of an American journey. When the offers came and I had to decide between a few competitive schools in the USA, I soon realized the strong hand of the most high on my life. How the travel expenses were going to be covered became an issue, but it was an opportunity I could not afford to lose. Many of my close associates disappointed me by discouraging me about the prospects of making it to the USA without money. I pressed on until a divine arrangement solved the problem effortlessly. By the time I even realized it, I was on my way to the USA. It was a special moment of fulfillment. I felt on top of the world.

Arrival in the USA was not what I had expected. There was so much adjustment to make and I realized the process may take time, which was normal. Though my communication with Lúcia kept me sane, I had to face the reality of my mission to succeed. Against all odds, the American dream took twice as much time to achieve, shook me off my strong foundation, and taught me to become even more determined in my quest for the Golden Fleece. What I lost in comfort from past habits, I gained in heightened thirst for knowledge. It did not come easily, though. A new person had to be forged. New habits had to be formed. Old attitudes had to give way to a fresh way of thinking. The American system felt individualistic. People kept to themselves. People minded their business. The collective sense of community was gone. Individualism and competition suddenly became a part of my system. I was gradually becoming a new person. It did not happen overnight, but came with cultural assimilation. Along the way, I met friendly and thoughtful people. When things go wrong, as they sometimes do, the human instinct tends to blame and judge. My negative experiences cultivated a habit of criticism in me. I was quick to judge people. I am reminded of the biblical admonition: "Judge not, that ye be not judged. For with what judgment ye judge, ye shall be judged: and with what measure ye mete, it shall be measured to you again (Matthew 7:1-2)."[4] As much as one would like to meditate on this counsel, human nature is but a weak vessel. It thrives on the imperfections of others in order to justify its own inadequacies. It is easy to blame others. It is difficult to look inward and see one's own shortcomings because no one is perfect. Yet self-reflection does have its limits. What hurts is this same human nature is also capable

---

4   https://codes.findlaw.com/il/chapter-720-criminal-offenses/il-st-sect-720-5-12-3-05.html. Accessed July 28, 2018.

of discriminating against others. My American journey is filled with different moods and moments, highs and lows. As I weighed the odds, I realized that if not for the glory of God, I would not have made it to this moment of grandeur. The past is history but the future is my destiny. Despite the many stumbling blocks, , I celebrate the life of Lúcia for hers is intertwined with mine and by giving me such memories now is part of a shining legacy that I still do not understand.

As a survivalist, I achieved the impossible. Lúcia may not be alive to enjoy the accomplishments with me, but she was the reason I survived. I would be seen as ungrateful to simply say she played her divine role as a supporter as she was supposed to. Yet, it was not enough a show of gratitude on my part to think that way. I feel as if writing this creative memoir is the best show of gratitude I could achieve for her. The road was long and tortuous. Many detractors played the role of destiny twisters, but they stumbled and fell. Something sustained my ambition despite all the odds. It was a vision. The vision may have been masked by nay-sayers who are nothing but observers of life. In the end, I was schooled in the struggles of life. I learnt to persevere and to remain undeterred. I learnt to look the other way during moments of anguish and hopelessness. I learnt to believe in the power of the mind. I learnt to pursue the power of vision. Above all, I put into action the many projects that naysayers thought were impossible. I completed my education and earned a doctorate degree. I survived the tenure-track travails. I have entered the gates of divine security that not even the gates of hell can stop. What remains is to ensure that no one else goes through this unnecessary delay of destiny in the pursuit of the American dream. *Lift up your heads, O ye gates; and be ye lift up, ye everlasting doors…* (Psalm 24:7). The moment is now.

6

Contemplations

Vera Barbosa ©
Barbosa Archives 2000

I had completely given up on seeing Lúcia ever again (except in another life), when she suddenly came visiting like a ghost. I did not realize that through dreams, it was possible to activate the human consciousness and cause a powerful spiritual reencounter with a loved one. It was early on a Sunday morning when she arrived. I had spent the days before in deep meditation after visiting my son, whom I had not seen in 10 years, for a whole week. Perhaps that visitation was a trigger. I would not know. I had spent an entire summer reflecting on the significance of this long departed human encourager of special destinies. I had written all I thought I remembered about her and her being. However, for some strange reason, my human energy was beginning to fail me. Then came the Buffalo Woman in a different form. She came as an angel on a mysterious mission. The entire house was filled with her overwhelming presence. I was transported to a new place and space where kaleidoscopic illuminations were the mood of the moment. Stupefied and speechless upon seeing her, she came reassuring me that it was truly her and not to be afraid. I summoned the courage to resist the encounter but I was overpowered by her sheer presence, grace, delight, and tranquility. Though I could see her shining figurative self, I could not touch her as she seemed no longer made of flesh and blood. Radiating all over her, was a special twilight covering that beats my imagination. It is true that many of us dream but not all of us remember in absolute recall. In the realm of the spirit, Lúcia crept into my consciousness to remind me of the past. As she moved me from the unconscious to the subconscious to consciousness, many energies and memories were transferred to me through the subconscious mind—provoking magical realism contained in infinite intelligence; a motivational encouragement that was responsible for the accomplishment of today. Through prolonged meditation across the Atlantic, cosmic energy releases transformative energies through which the mind, the body, and the spirit commingle in a complex fluidity of infinite intelligence.

In submitting to the illuminating potentialities of the empowering spirit realm, I tap into the verities Lúcia has come to share through archetypal revelations. As I struggle to make sense of the dreams, the departed soul takes me to a higher level—asking and answering questions that I could not even comprehend myself. Like a seed that goes dormant, I died many times to this physical body through the tortuous journeys of life. Little did I know that the different challenges were a gradual preparation for the spiritual manifestation of my better subconscious. Dreaming may be a channel of recuperating memory when the past is remembered; but in the case of Lúcia, she becomes a catalyst to the greater dimension of the spiritual realm when the physical is so tortured that it wants to forget those painful memories from the past. I wish things could have unraveled differently as if part of me was apologetic for betraying the unspoken pact of my return to Brazil much sooner than it actually materialized. I felt Lúcia had to visit me in the spiritual realm to relieve me of my concerns that it was not my fault that I could not be there at her moment of frailty. Not in the same way she was there for me. Lúcia harbored no such feelings of accusation or blame. Rather, I was the one feeling guilty for the present state of affairs that she had come to lay to rest. She actually made me comfortable and at peace. I was a little scared of her presence despite her efforts to tranquilize me. I was not sure if she simply came to settle the score or simply respond to our missing links in communication that probably drifted sometime between the end of one semester and the beginning of the other. After reassuring me that her visit was meant as resolving "unfinished business" of peace and tranquility, I regained confidence and opened myself up to what she had to share. I will now let the rest of these cosmic contemplations speak through the voice of Lúcia as she has requested. After all, she is the only one who can fill the gaps after so many years of absence.

I, Lúcia, speak with the tranquility of the ancients amidst the troubled streams of the terrestrial world... From my remote supernatural abode, I felt your weariness as you tried to reconstruct our cosmic communication. Be not afraid nor be dismayed. I have come to assist you in your efforts to remember. There is so much to remember and I hope my faculty of remembrance serves me well. I have come to relive our memorable times together without interfering with your own sense of peace. It was only last Friday night in October that I received your communication. I could not reply on Saturday because I would have had to wait until Monday to mail it anyway. And so I waited till Sunday to write. There are many things I want to talk about. I truly do not know where to begin. I think I will start with the last issue of your letter. In your last mail, you mentioned that you deliberately suppressed what you called the "big problem" that afflicted you in Chicago and you wondered if I was sad or worried. You may have received other communication regarding my own frame of mind then but let me reiterate my feelings. I was not really as saddened or worried about the problems, but more concerned with your state of mind. Remember, I had wanted you to tell me more about your soul even without knowing the nature of the problem. That was my telepathic message in action! I also felt that someone must be interfering with our communication by stealing the letters. I am not naïve. Something is not adding up, but here I am with you now to set the record straight. For you, as you claimed then, the "big problem" was over, but not quite so for me. I think even now you are still living this problem psychologically. Perhaps for not having someone close by from your culture to talk to or perhaps not having me close to you during the ordeal. I wonder if it is permissible for me to be so pretentious of my significance in your life? Even if you had someone by your side at that troubling time, some things would still have been very difficult to resolve. In my opinion, I think everything worked out for the best. You needed to find yourself, believe in yourself, strengthen yourself, grow, and learn to dribble in life all by yourself. Thereafter, of course it would be helpful for someone else to be with you to help put things in the proper perspective. It must all start from you.

I believe that you will overcome all the odds once you overcome the psychological impact of the culture shock you were experiencing. The routine of classes, work, and even the corrections on your exams and quizzes, must be seen in a positive manner. They all constitute a normal struggle for a decent and honest lifestyle that makes one happy. You must learn to dominate time in order to balance things, get your work done, and still have time left for creativity and other activities that help you fulfill your moments of leisure. Consider time as your friend and not as your enemy. By being yourself, having fun with your students, challenging them, enjoying their answers to your questions, and enriching the curious ones, you actually learn from the process and from your students. What I sense from our communication is that you are constantly suffering due to human conflicts when you could be happy in spite of them. Whether it is with your own assignments, research, teaching, disappointments, or not having love and affection close by, you sound like you are barely holding yourself together and could give it all up at any moment. I hope that is not the case. Every change is indeed a shock! You must know that such a shock was inevitable in a new environment. Consequently, I did not expect that you would allow such events to profoundly affect you in the negative. You cannot afford to allow events to push you to the corner. If you succumb to such pressures, then you lose control of everything. You will not be able to cope with your normal daily rhythm, may always be late with everything, and begin to make excuses for not getting your work done. You need to get yourself out of this anguished frame of mind.

As you get rid of your negative thinking, you need to breathe in and out and say enough is enough to these unfortunate inner conflicts that translate into insecurities and accumulated daily assignments. I hope you will not regret my sharing my thoughts with you and stop communicating with me. You need not stop sharing your ideas with me. Let us keep sharing ideas and not constant personal conflicts. By nature, conflicts are in phases and not a daily event that drains us of vital energy. Now that your life has returned to normalcy, seek to document your experiences and observations without letting them weigh you down. Otherwise, the negative thoughts that are part of human nature will always find you at your weakest moments. Learn to resist them. Before going to another matter, I saw the photo you sent from Chicago. You looked so beaten down though you were forcing a smile. You were seemingly happy for having won the case, but you still looked not quite yourself. May I ask you for a favor? No matter what you are going through, I want you to take good care of your nutrition. Eat well, eat balanced and nutritional food all the time. Never use work and stress as excuses not to eat well. You once inquired if your spontaneities in your communication bothered me? Never. Your communication is always expected with much affection and positive anxiety. Rather, my concern is if you actually believe in yourself based on your occasional expression of doubts. I am more interested in how you resolve issues and not necessarily in you not sharing your feelings with me out of fear of my using your words against you. Even when you keep things to yourself, I can always feel the energy when things are wrong. I would rather you keep communicating.

You once stated that the assignments were steadily accumulating. Of course, that is to be expected because you failed to get them done! You did not get them done because you gave up on yourself. You seemed to have a strategy of focusing on just *one* thing at a time. Is that what you call being episodic? Darling, learn the principle of multi-tasking. I understand what you went through in Chicago was traumatic. Yet, this is not the first time you gave up on getting your work done. You have a frame of mind that is strangely episodic. Is it because you felt you were living in a foreign country? You have been traveling the world for no less than ten years. You are a well-seasoned traveler. You should be used to the cultural differences in the countries you have lived in and people you have met. I think you need to get in tune with yourself, with your acute sensibility, and your excessive sensibility to be specific!

You need to get to know yourself better; discover the extent to which you want to be sensitive so that this attitude does not keep affecting you but rather work in your favor. That way, you master the art of knowing when to talk, when to be quiet, where to go, who to avoid, when to write, and when to reflect and strategize. Let your sensibility work positively for you. By synchronizing sensibility and reason, you will ultimately have a balance, a sense of harmony to be precise, by uniting your soul and spirit in order to cope with a system you have described as cold. You need to keep talking to people so you do not isolate yourself unnecessarily. You have a talkative nature but instead of talking about things that commit you to intensity, discover how to talk about the weather, rain, and shine, just to escape people wasting your time that you need to get your work done. The incident in the plane may have been provoked by your natural and persistent need to talk to strangers. If you had avoided talking to that little white girl, you probably would have avoided any contact or consequence.

As part of your survival strategies, you may have to come to terms with the fact that you are in a new system and must adapt yourself. If life is individualistic and programmatic in the USA, it is because you are dealing with a developed country with its own technical, electronic, and mechanical dispositions. Since you are already used to this from your travel experiences, you should not let it bother you so much or suffer because of the change in environment. By accepting to study in such a system, you have also accepted the conditionality's. If you were to go to the Amazonia, the conditions would be completely different such as you would expect in an underdeveloped country. You wonder about the "freedom" that is propagated about the USA if people are not really "free" but that is your own perception or opinion. You may be frustrated by your unfortunate experiences but that is the price we pay in order to come to terms with the truth. I do not think you are enjoying my frank reflections. I just do not think you need me to mask anything up for you. Rather, I am being very direct and honest with you. I am not even being poetic except for bringing you to a realistic resonance with the American reality in which you live. We can even be a little poetic, sensitive, loving, but with people we are so close, like family and intimate friends, people in whom we cast all our trust, people with whom we can be more direct and sincere. I hope this is beginning to make sense to you? I just want you to know that I love you very much! I will only become relieved of your worries and be happy after knowing that you have somehow dealt with your existential conflicts, your seeming lack of security, your lack of trust in others, and your ability to overcome the odds without letting these passing challenges affect your inner spirit. Take good care of your inner being. You are an example of a strong, lively, and sensitive human being.

By the way, you never imagined how tough my life is, too. You never bothered to ask about how I coped with daily challenges, with my son, what it takes living with my mother, father, and brother under the same roof, even at my age? It is very difficult… very, very, difficult. Can you imagine how I cope with school, the demands of my family, and how I ever have time left to do anything for myself? My family always expects me to do something for them; things to which I cannot say no. Yet, I must create time for me, for my school work, and also give attention to everyone around me. You think I do not have issues to deal with? I surely do. You think I am never broke?

I surely am. The question is how I cope with it all? I cope by loving myself, believing in myself, and never giving up. Since my goal is to complete my studies, I will go all the way to the end. It is good in all the senses: professionally and also as a great example for my son to emulate. I have within me the Infinite Energy. I also have God. If I do not believe in myself, who is going to believe in me? If I do not help myself, who is going to be willing to help me, even if they want to? I cope by loving myself, believing in myself, professing positive statements: I am happy; problems disappear from me even before I perceive them as such. Problems make me sad for a few moments and soon enough, I radiate love, joy, security, and happiness to all; I have no time to dwell on negativity.

Beyond my immediate family, I also have to cater to the needs of my colleagues at work. We are nine in all. I have to convince and understand my boss, who is very insecure and who aspires to be a star, and thus maltreats those wishing to meet with him. I never miss work. I wake up as early as 6AM to get ready and prepare my son for the day. I am also kind to you in my thoughts every day. I do the best I can for my extended family in the same house. I arrive at work and the rhythm begins: with phone calls, appointments to make, pending matters to resolve, and wish for a quick peace of mind during lunch time? It is very difficult to balance it all. And when I go to any restaurant within the University of São Paulo, I meet a wide range of diverse people who want to chat with me. When they are not Nigerians or from other African countries, they are new arrivals on campus wishing to forge new friendships. Then it gets complicated as I do not want any close friendship, but I also do not want to be misunderstood. Hence, I always find a way to escape or avoid unwanted advances. By the time I look at the clock later on in the afternoon, it is time to go to my evening school where I have seminars to present or assignments to submit. When do I have time to prepare them all? Yet, I still have to wash my clothes, pick my son from school, prepare him dinner or if time was an issue, eat out and take him with me to school. Tell me Clétus, how do I perform the miracle of dribbling time? I must either make time, my friend, or keep suffering. I accept my life as it is; common like anyone else's, but different because I am at peace with myself. Alas! I do have my moments of sadness. The solution is not to dwell on it. It is only a flash of the moment. Soon enough, the sadness passes. I do not let it control my life.

You often say you will try to make me happy. Oh no! Don't just try! Make me happy please, Clétus. Believe in yourself as much as you believe in me. You have unique opportunities that many do not have and are still struggling to have. Therefore, take advantage of your privileged position. I know you worked hard for these opportunities and are deserving of them, but you are not even allowing yourself to enjoy them. You are allowing negative forces to overtake your spirit due to a mere traumatic distraction. You seem to be vulnerable to external spiritual influences. Resist, henceforth, the diabolic forces that are trying to derail your well-being and compromise your destiny. You also appreciate me for giving you vital energy to keep on going. Thank God that I am able to fulfill this role of spiritual empowerment. I am glad to have helped you grow spiritually, believe more in yourself, and become a complete human being and different man—not a man-machine. You need to be strong to counter all human inequalities without allowing them to touch your inner spirit so profoundly. Only take away whatever each experience brings to you in the positive to enrich your life. You also mention that you reach out to me a lot in your subconscious since my words or our words serve as a therapeutic mystery to you due to being so far away. Yet, I believe that such need to communicate with a loved one should not affect you negatively. Rather, it should encourage you even more. In other words, why are we both sacrificing our time and energies? Should it not all be for a greater outcome and purpose in the future? And, not necessarily a permanent state of suffering? Of course, a little suffering is fine, but ultimately there has to be some worthwhile light at the end of the tunnel. Otherwise, it is better to let everything go, right?

I wonder why you have become so pessimistic? You wonder if better moments will return as we had in Brazil. I should be asking why you allowed a simple incident affect you so much that it changed everything about your worldview? Even if everyone is crazy in this world today, there is bound to be better days ahead. By affirming this positive attitude, we are able to project a better future. What is important is to focus on what is positive. Just consider our cosmic communication. How many people sustain this kind of utopian exchanges? Of course, for us it is real, it is reality, it is not utopian at all. Our communication is something very valuable, profound, and rare. Is all of this not beautiful? Are they not great moments to behold and share? And when we meet again, how beautiful would that be since we would have gotten to know each other very profoundly! We will be better prepared and more mature than before. Do you now see that there are better moments ahead of us and things will not always be negative? Let me make an appeal to you: let us assume we truly live amidst crazy folks in an insane world, let us do everything to take care of each other so as not to become crazy as well. That way, we will be well-prepared for the era of Aquarius. When you mentioned that you went to church to thank God for the relief in Chicago, I was very pleased. We need to show gratitude for all God does for us: our health and for both negative and positive experiences we gain by passing through them. And, most importantly, for learning to grow in the process. You keep referencing the Chicago affair but instead of seeing it as a mystery, it is better to face it as a manifestation of misunderstanding that we must learn to live with as black people living in what appears to be a white world.

As a matter of fact, the mystery I see in all of this is that you are a free man today because the Higher Forces were with you and protected you. Things could have turned out even worse than you expected. Perhaps they saw you as a risk, someone to check out at entry in case he belongs to a suspicious group that needs to be domesticated right away. Who knows? The mystery remains that the system did bite its tongue and realized that they made a serious mistake. It was shameful, yes, but it was their own shame. It was a case of racial prejudice. It is nice to see you express that you are regaining your sense of excitement, confidence, and liveliness all over again. You also wanted to know how it would be if I were living with you. Yes, we are thinking the same way. It crossed my mind the same way. Can you imagine how lovely that would be?

Let me just surprise you: I plan to be with you in July of 1988 for a summer course in English only if I am able to save up for such a major venture. Otherwise, I don't know. In case it works out, I will need your help to select a class that lasts only for one month. I know it is usually intensive, maybe for 5 hours per-day maximum so that I can visit places; and also enjoy myself. I was wondering if I could also work but that may be impossible. I was just thinking of my own professional development; being able to do what I do here in English instead of in Portuguese to which I am accustomed. Despite the competition, I would like to give it a try. I want to be able to look into people's faces and see how ridiculous it is that they are thinking they will not die like everyone else. They may not even realize I would be making fun of them in my own way. Do let me know of such a possibility as soon as possible. I know there is never going to be an end to this saga but as I contemplate a real visit close to you in the summer, let me share André and Matheus's music (Sem Você Não Viverei[1] [Without You I am Lifeless]) which provides

---

1   https://codes.findlaw.com/il/chapter-720-criminal-offenses/il-st-sect-720-5-12-3-05.html. Accessed July 28, 2018.

consolation to me as well, even as I try to encourage you: "Ou, ou, ou, ei, ei, ei / Without you I am lifeless / Return soon as I cannot cope / With this distance from you… / My heart is urging you / to return soon my love." Even as I do everything to fill this void, I am also energized about tomorrow. I begin to contemplate what a future with you will be like. Another song comes to mind in the lyrics of Simone in "O Amanhã"[2] [Tomorrow]): "What is tomorrow going to be like? / Whomever knows should answer me / What is going to happen to me? / My destiny shall be / As God wants it." With these two songs, I remind you of all I have been repeating as telepathic messages: take good care of your nutrition, resist negative energies, avoid being mentally contaminated by your environment, and always believe in yourself.

You may be getting upset with me for stressing the issue of your personal conduct and responsibility as you address the challenges you are facing in a new environment. I know the semester is coming to an end for you and for me and I appreciate your finding time to communicate with me despite your stressful situation. You had threatened to stop writing to me based on my using your words against you. I confess that was not my intention. Your anger towards me will subside when you calm down to understand my intentions. I also understand your side of things—sadness that I am not saying what you want to hear. I am sure in the future you will understand my cold, indifferent, frank, and provocative words. My goal is very precise: I would like you to be able to make the best decisions for yourself during tough indecisive moments. I just hate to see you suffering so much. I know you are a very sensitive person; yet on the other hand, we have to deal with the reality of the wild world we live in. I do not see all human beings as bestial. I can tell you for sure that the worst animal on the face

---

2   https://codes.findlaw.com/il/chapter-720-criminal-offenses/il-st-sect-720-5-12-3-05.html. Accessed July 28, 2018.

of the planet is man. I would urge you not to be so upset with me. I would rather you positively analyze the nuances of my reactions to your painful experiences that you were sharing with me. In order to fully understand what you were going through and provide a candid response that you needed, I needed to provoke you through my questions and analysis. Who else would understand me if not you? If I cannot get you to understand me, then I would simply give up on humanity. After all, I am human with my own limitations as well. I am sure this is a passing challenge for both of us; and I can see you appreciating my supportive role as we move forward in our relationship.

As I reflect on the issues we have discussed in the last month or so, I can see some efforts on your part to reintegrate yourself even more within the system by reaching out to African and Brazilian constituencies. This makes me very happy. When it comes to your health, I can only hope that you are taking good care of yourself as much as possible because you have to be healthy in order to function well. I am also relieved to see that despite the challenges you are passing through, you keep invoking my being the flower in your life. I am overwhelmed with the resolve to counter the negative energies and find your positive bearing against the odds. If for any reason, you feel you have done everything possible and you feel like the system is trying to destroy your peace and harmony, then it seems to me that your only alternative is to leave the country. I know this is a last resort of sorts and you are not the one to do that, I am just trying to see how determined you are to fulfil your objectives. I am also transported to the shifting states of your mind as I revisit the chronology of your subconscious manifestations since you arrived in the USA. It was nice to see that while it was difficult to adapt, you made Herculean efforts to return to normalcy after the scary event in Chicago. By remaining busy, you overcame the humiliating and ridiculous episode and felt like a winner after it was all over. You are being strong; frankly, I am not sure if I would have been able to cope with such a discriminatory situation. Though you bonded with Brazilians, it was as if it was the last resort left for you. I appreciate your words of appreciation and dedication, and I love you even more as the days pass. You are unique and I am very proud of you. Let me share some words of James Baldwin with you: "Not everything we confront can be changed, but nothing can be changed if not confronted."[3] I am pleased and privileged to know that I am the only one you are sharing your inner secrets with. It makes me feel very special.

Let me return to the issue of your health. When we go through accumulated traumatic incidents, one after the other, there is a tendency for the health to suffer. I am sure you are fine, but when I received your strange communication with the envelope of Brasília, I almost thought you were back in Brazil. I see you as a very transcendental human being who can be in many places all at the same time. You give me hope, too, in humanity. You are like a warring horse that is fearless and determined to overcome all odds. We will always have challenges but we must also take control over circumstances. Consider the example of Mandela. Will he ever be free from prison? Imagine what he sacrificed and what his entire family sacrificed? It is as if he went to jail with them. Are you following the news about him at all? You should follow his activities so that when he is released you can appreciate the sacrifices he made and use that to encourage yourself that even ideological goals come with serious sacrifice. I also want to hint at the potential for laziness. This may not be your case as I have known you to be very hardworking. I am referring to the possibility of distractions. Things in Brazil are getting worse. President Reagan plans to cut off our exports and that means Brazil may

---

3   https://codes.findlaw.com/il/chapter-720-criminal-offenses/il-st-sect-720-5-12-3-05.html. Accessed July 28, 2018.

enter into economic recession. Reagan is pushing this agenda just because Brazil is becoming self-sufficient especially in the area of information technology. How can Brazil survive if we as a people do not come together to unite to resist this American imperialism? I have no doubt in my mind that the weight of the problems you are facing right now will surely provoke creative solution from you and let you realize how important professional development is to you. I believe in you; never give up! You know exactly how to motivate me as well. Should you want to return to Brazil forever, or for vacation, I am here for you, my love. Only you can make me happy. Only you…

    That was how she vanished without a trace. Since her departure, I have always wondered when she will return to keep me company. My entire being was locked in the nexus of nostalgia.

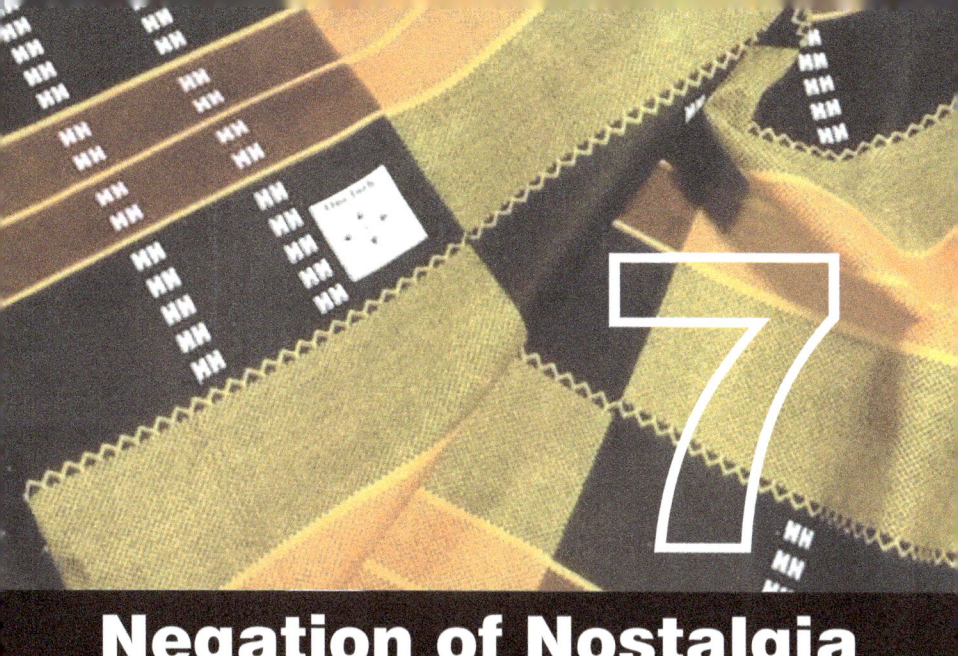

7
Negation of Nostalgia

Vera Barbosa
© Barbosa Archives 1982

Lúcia's recent mysterious apparition has been magical in its direct frankness—touching on many issues that border around survival strategies and facing one's fears and doubts in the midst of a set strategic objective. It was an opportunity for her to do what she does best: console, encourage, and motivate even if through tough enunciations and analyses. On both sides, what keeps motivating us to maintain this cosmic communication is how it helps us cope with nostalgia. Much of what I wanted to tell her was about missing her, about how tough life was and how her being far away was affecting me psychologically. I could not find love and compassion in anyone else as our relationship was emotionally deep and invested. Knowing what I know about her for many years, I felt like comparing her to others I have met in the USA and with whom I have not had such intimate moments. Also at this same moment in time, my grades from the previous semester arrived. I was finding out that a Brazilian professor had given me all As in his classes while the third class, taught by an American professor, had turned out to be below my expectation. I wanted to share the wickedness of the American professor with Lúcia, but the correspondence takes forever between two continents and I couldn't wait for her guidance. I protested the discriminatory treatment within me and promised myself that no one would ever discourage me from my defined goal. I was beginning to feel the pressure of adjustment to the American educational system, and factoring in the possibility of racism and double standards. Despite the possibility of proving myself anew in the following semester, I was getting some mixed messages about possibly returning to Brazil at the end of the academic year. I did not want it to be a self-fulfilling prophecy. I was imagining scenarios of being together with Lúcia, not to escape the reality of the USA but as a psychological succor from a feeling of being backed into a frustrating corner. Even without personal funds to finance the trip, I was even beginning to encourage her to come on a summer visit to the USA as previously discussed. Is this not just wishful thinking on my part? When am I going to wake up from my perpetual slumber? Such was the moment of reality that required an attempt to negate nostalgia. Suddenly, the apparition continues at the right moment of need. Lúcia appears to keep my anxieties under some needed control. I was relieved.

I, Lúcia, speak in the name of Fulfillment of Destinies... I have heard of your worries and queries and I am back to provide answers to your perpetual wonderings. Fortunately, your need to communicate is as intense as mine... it is mutual. Everyone seeks happiness through many means: drugs, money, travels, love, career, family, etc. I don't think one should be sad about your present condition because in order to have balance in this world once must be ready to take the good with the bad: death and life; love and hate. However, one needs not suffer perpetually. I am not delighted that you find yourself in this game of life. You need to take care of yourself, be strong, understand the imbalances of life and forge towards reaching out for a balance. Let's take the case of your professor that you find rather discriminatory. You can always use this challenge to prove to her and yourself, that despite the odds, you can be victorious. You may not have gotten what you expected from her as recompense, but you did better than most people in your situation would have done. You not only won the small battles, you also won the war. If you set a higher goal within the circumstances, you could have gone crazy. That would have been a self-fulfilling prophecy. I urge you to congratulate yourself for a job well-done. Stop trying to be a perfectionist. This illusion does not exist. It is better to take things easy; one step at a time. You should, in fact, be giving yourself some credit for overcoming such a challenging situation.

Beyond these passing distractions that you have handled well, I feel your presence all around me as if you are speaking to my ears. When we feel each other's expression of love, with so much passion and intensity, only to sleep and wake up so far away from each other... Is it worth it? Beyond the wish to cry each morning due to nostalgia, there is a permanent melancholy that emanates from the distance that separates us. It will only be worthwhile if you can return in one piece; and not so brutalized in your heart and mind. At times, I feel like telling you that, in your search for greener pastures in the USA, you have traded the human and the spiritual in you for the material world. It was a good decision, don't get me wrong, but you must deal with the consequences without regrets. You are actually in a privileged position. You can still smile and feel good about yourself. Don't you follow the news from other countries and the condition of other people? Don't you see and hear about hunger, torture, and deaths in other socio-political systems? Would you rather go to war for your country? Sacrifice your life? Do you want to find yourself in a country where you are obliged to take up arms against innocent children and women? Things could be much worse, my dear. Don't you hear about Haiti where innocent children are being mutilated? What about working in the gold mines of South Africa? Do you want to be forced to walk in the battlefield to see if there are dangerous mines on the ground? You should be grateful to God for being so blessed and privileged. By weighing the possibilities of things being worse, you will truly appreciate what you have despite the challenges. You need to wake up and take advantage of the opportunities you have. When are you going to wake up to smell the roses? Have you ever thought things could be worse? Things can actually be worse for you, believe me. Why must it get to this point? There is no point threatening to stop communicating with me. It is you who must change your way of thinking and see things more positively.

    Candidly, millions of people would like to trade places with you. Many would like to take your place as a privileged African in the USA. Stop seeing only the negative side of things. Stop wanting to be perfect and demanding perfection in life. Wake up and grow up young man! Instead of investing only in books of poetry, start reading and understanding humanity. Just think of those who lived through slavery. Perhaps you want to be a slave to your own thinking? Your fixed ideas? Your pleasure of suffering? Is this how you change the world? I don't like when you suggest that I am strong and you are suffering. Are you suggesting that you like to suffer? That you are a radical being? I doubt it if you know what suffering is. You probably do not want to know. My struggle is not describable. At the end of the semester, when I look at myself in the mirror, I hardly believe it was me. A whole different person. I feel completely wasted that it was impossible to return to the person I used to be. But I never suffered any heartache due to this. My pain was only physical; resultant of tiredness, and a struggle that I was already aware of before getting started with the degree program in Tourism and Management. I had to submit to the rules of the game I bargained for. My concern all along, as I followed your struggles in the USA, was that if you were to show up at my house unannounced for example; and knocked at the door and you were to say: "Please, does Lúcia live here?" You will be the one who is shocked. How can we ever be sure how I was going to respond to the situation? I am suggesting a scenario where you left the USA abruptly to return to be with me in Brazil. We may be back to square one of rejection and confusion, and there was no way of knowing. Everything in life has a price. If things are not working, it is probably because that is not what you wanted all along and it is time to pursue a different objective. Enough of stressing yourself, young man! Change your thinking so as not to receive the punishment of God for not appreciating what you have. You are so perfect in body and soul. You just need to change your thinking and stop suffering.

    Now, let's stop suffering together and talk about better things of life. You are yet to tell me about the black community in the USA. What about your extended family in Africa? What about your so-called roommate? Of course, I am serious about my summer plan to visit you and I will see things for myself. Imagine those who are blind or have one leg or arm? Are they complaining like you? Is God not being generous to you by creating you as a complete human being and yet you are not grateful by complaining about your situation? Yet, the months are passing by so fast. Even the New Year is only two weeks away. You have brought new perspective to my life. Soon, I will be with you. I am beginning to live a full life. It feels like I was born anew and only now I am waking up to that reality. Today is Sunday. My family would normally go to the *Camisa Verde e Branco* [White and Green Shirt] School of Samba. Where are you, Clétus? Would you not like to go with me to enjoy dancing samba? I envisage that with time, your life will start changing and you will become famous. I urge you not to leave me out of this life of victory. I love you so much. In case I said some harsh things, in case I made some negative comments in context so that you can wake up into your destiny, I seek your forgiveness so that we can grow together in love. Remember all we did together in São Paulo before you travelled? Remember how I took you to my family the very first day? Before we move into other issues, let me provide you with some stimulating and quotable sayings: (i) Every day I wake up in order to win; (ii) There is neither a wrong nor a right way but what is possible; (iii) I do not want to waste my time under the bed covers listening to nonsense. I prefer to listen to interesting and useful things; (iv) Only God and I are capable of making something out of nothing; (v) There are no favorable winds for a naval officer who does not know his destination (vi) One should never confuse an erotic impulse with that of love; (vii) A man only fails when he stops trying; and (viii) I never needed an alarm clock to wake up. With these motivational tips, I hope you can come to terms with positive thinking and resolve your inner doubts.

Just like you, a series of exams is ahead of me and I have to prepare for them. I am now close to the end of the semester but communicating with you is my vital and primordial priority. The only reason this cosmic communication is sustained is because we have infinite feelings, affinities, and objectives in common. We cannot afford to lose this unique experience and moment. It is divine. Kindly let me preface my next spontaneities with some reflections: be comfortable with yourself and any decision you make by the end of the academic year in terms of whether you want to continue where you are now or you want to make another bold decision about your future—be it in the USA or in Brazil. Weigh your options very well, and ask whether you want to be alone or you want to be with someone else and *where* exactly in the world. I know you have an achievement orientation, thus I am not worried about your success. I like the way you address me as "beloved" or "darling." It makes me feel very important, like a princess to you. All my efforts to date center around encouraging you to the point where you regain your self-esteem and security and to ensure that you do not regret any decision you have made or will soon make. As you counter the negative energies of the people you come in contact with, with positive vibrations, you become spiritually stronger. I know you cannot communicate as constantly as you were doing before due to assignments that are accumulating, but as long as you make an effort, I will understand. Through dialogue, harmony and peace, we will overcome this stress of distance and nostalgia. Through our communication, we are actually coping with the sense of frustration that we cannot be together as much as we wish. You talk a lot about Curuzu in Salvador where Ilê Aiyê Afro-Carnival organization is located, but I am still waiting for you to take me there with you—so we can be there together. I also remember all about São Paulo that we discovered together: On Campus, the New Administration Building, Languages and Literatures Department, School of Communication, African Studies, the Main Library, and all I desire is for you to be back in my arms. Am I sleepwalking or just dreaming? I hope not. You mean everything to me, dear.

When I was younger, I used to write short stories and novellas. Even my father had this tendency. He once wrote a play. If I were to take writing seriously today, I would write about my vision on sex and religion. I would also write another on the use of our mind. But I am not as experienced a writer as you for I am sure writing about these issues would make me so sad as I contemplate the dubious character of humans living on this earth. It is a whole mess to think about this entire human species—so bastardized, deceived, killing and exploring each other. When I consider the exploitative set of white people who treat men and women as shit. Worse still, women suffer even more than men because men think they are superior to women and treat women as trash, objects, and material collections. This is what leads to the confusion and chaos in the world. Man is yet to accept himself and know himself through respect and love. It is a very stupid attitude. And this is why we have what we have today: millions suffering from sexually transmitted diseases such as AIDS, mental illnesses, and other human oppressions. You may not like the competition, the mechanized way of life, and the lack of human warmth as you see it, but you have to adapt to the reality because it is like that everywhere though in varying degrees. I appreciate your seeing me as God-sent by my disposition towards you. My words, like yours, carry such transformative power that I am beginning to see you as a golden heart. You are as bright as the heavens and I hope you can see yourself in the same positive light as you see me. Amidst a multitude, you are unique; you shine and you are a divine light. I appreciate you as well.

Though you occasionally hint at the possibility of returning to Brazil, or the possibility of my joining you in the USA, the decision making process is neither here or there. I feel both of us are perambulating, but the desire to see each other is strong and genuine. Part of me feels it is just a nostalgic thing and that you may not really mean it. How can I simply abandon my family? It is a serious decision that will affect both of us. I know you're getting a teaching job in Brazil will not be an issue. You are more than qualified. You are fluent and competent in many languages, including English that is well in demand here in Brazil. My main concern is what all that means for my family and for my job. It was very difficult for me to get to this point in my professional career as a Secretary of a Director of the Institute of Advanced Studies. My boss is white and insecure. He is one of the few whites that will put any trust in a black woman. Yet, I made it to the top of my secretarial career with huge sacrifices. Coming to the USA is a whole different story. It is a tough decision that I am excited about but also frightened. I am not so sure you are ready to take on another person into your unstable life when you are still struggling to adapt yourself within the American system. It may be too much burden for you. Besides, I am much older than you; and I am not sure how you will feel about that down the road. Living together under the same roof is not as easy as people think even when two people love each other. There are issues that we are not aware of right now that we are living apart that will come up. And, what about my son? What will become of him? If I am coming to join you, I guess he will stay behind in Brazil first. Then how easy will that be for me to be away from my son? I am not sure I can handle that. I am not sure I am ready for that. Maybe you are ready since you get along with him anyway. Yet, getting along on a short-term visit is not the same as living together permanently under the same roof with so many responsibilities that we cannot take for granted.

Let me give you my candid suggestion. Think about what is best for your happiness and consequently the happiness of everyone. As far as I am concerned, we should live either where the wife was born or where the husband was born. I am not comfortable with the idea of us living in the USA and selfishly, I even prefer to live in Brazil. Why not complete your studies first before deciding where to live? Let's live our lives with joy as life is too short. You may not like hearing this—life is passing you by and all you think about is books and books alone. In case you return to Brazil before completing your degree, what would you do? Teach? Study? We would need to buy a house or rent for a while. Rent has gone up 200%. Everyone is crazy now regarding economic survival. Within 15 days, cost of gasoline has increased twice. There is definitely a recession in Brazil right now. Everyone is complaining. Are you really prepared to live as a married couple? Won't you suffer the crisis of sudden change? I am worried by the consequences. Living as a couple is not easy. What if you fall in love with someone else? I am talking from experience, love. You need to think deeply about this decision. It is not funny. Let me add a caution. It is more difficult to separate than to initiate this living arrangement. Knowing that you are so sensitive the same way that I am, it would be very painful if anyone of us were to regret the decision. I actually think you are better off returning to Brazil, live by yourself for a short while, until you decide what you really want for your life. What do you think? At times, I get the sense that you still do not know what you really want for your life. You once indicated coming back to Brazil in December or January. Later you stated you wanted to go to Washington to continue your studies. At times, I do not understand your thinking. Imagine us being together for just one month. And soon enough, you may meet someone else and become confused.

Beloved, I have so much love, affection, and patience for you. Although you claim that I am more experienced, I still feel so naïve; you can confirm this in your own heart as well, and I know God is with me all the way; hence, I keep on living. Yes, I have all these things you feel that I have but I still have moments that I feel like talking to someone about my anguish, my fears, and my pain. Are you not concerned? Are you not worried? Search profoundly within you; and do not be fooled by our intimate communication. Life as a couple is different from being far from one another when we have reason to contemplate and write to each other. When we are living together and you feel like communicating with another person by habit; who will you communicate with? It is not as if I am discouraging your plan or that I am not excited at the possibility of your coming to be with me, I just don't want you to be disappointed as you were by going to the USA. I want you to be sure and firm without any reservations that you want us to be together forever and ever. As a matter of fact, beyond our long term passion and love, I am beginning to see you as Brazilian. I also see myself as African as if I have lived in Africa before and shared your ancestral connections. I like your facial features that are close to mine to a certain degree. Are you Yoruba? You are so beautiful in name and color. Perhaps I am dreaming. At times, I always imagine carrying your child. Imagine having a son or daughter with your color, your expressive eyes, your smiles and your name. That would be wonderful… but I must wake up to the reality… we are yet to resolve this issue of distance between us.

    I completely understand your need to apologize for having insecure moments. Yet, you are not completely responsible for the course of events beyond your control. In my overall understanding, you were responding to the stimuli you encountered in your new setting. We all have moments of insecurity, fear, desires and needs, depending on the circumstances. I trust that you will definitely overcome. As long as you know what you want, nothing will stop you from attaining your objectives. The current situation is only a passing obstacle for you to truly define within your heart the path you want to take or renegotiate. Something that touched me the most was the moment you expressed the term "weakness." That is a serious word. I hope you are eating well and taking good care of your health. By being "weak," are you referring more to psychological weakness and not to the physical? If you are weak spiritually, then it means that all my words are not having any impact on you. When we are weak, we make the wrong decisions. I want you to take care of yourself in all possible ways. Even when you feel like giving up, you need to summon the courage to struggle and resist. Do not empower your own disillusionment by subscribing to negative thinking. You are strong. You are not weak. In my opinion, you must do everything to accelerate your degree program and complete it as fast as you can because with that on your CV, many opportunities will open up for you anywhere in the world. You must surprise your enemies and mischief-makers. Those who are calling you "monkey" today will soon kneel down right in front of you in due season to pay homage. They may be behaving like your enemies and detractors today, but they are also unconsciously pushing you towards fulfilling your destiny. I think you need to face the situation head-on, and not escape from the painful challenge. It is shameful and defeatist to run away from challenges in life. If you run away from this problem, you never know what other problems are waiting for you in the near future. Face this one as a man of courage and you will not regret it no matter what. Though Bob Marley says "he who fights and runs away, lives to fight another day,"[1] you have a unique opportunity to actually shame your enemies by fighting and not running away for this is a win or lose situation. If you

---

1 https://codes.findlaw.com/il/chapter-720-criminal-offenses/il-st-sect-720-5-12-3-05.html. Accessed July 28, 2018.

lose this battle, you may not have another chance to redeem yourself.

I am very convinced that by completing your challenging degree, you will grow professionally; and only growing in this way can you discover that the world is full of masks and actors, even as you yourself observed in your poem, "A pensive voice from room." Notwithstanding the challenges, your dream is not in any way unrealistic as long as you are determined and well aware that there is someone supporting you from far away and yet so close. I not only respect you, I also respect your dreams and goals and I feel as if we are in this struggle together despite the distance. All those who value others, will surely appreciate what happiness is, what peace signifies, and will do everything to join you in this intense pursuit of a desirable objective that will ultimately make you happy even though only few people will appreciate why you have to make such sacrifices. I like your deep analysis of past, present, and future. I get the sense that you are coming to terms with the value in believing that there is indeed light at the end of the tunnel. It feels good that you are turning around to be stronger and more resolved. Our communication has definitely changed in tone. It is now clearly romantic and magical. You totally convinced me that you are the only special being in my life. I had almost lost all hope of finding such a rare soulmate who would understand me in this world. I was searching for that special being who respects my qualities and understands me while forgiving my weaknesses as a human being. Alas, to the glory of God, from the blue, you came to show me the way, to assure me that someone like you still exists in this crazy world. In fact, I would like to be by your side all the time, in order to embrace and kiss you ceaselessly. One thing I must ask of you: Can you please let us forget the Chicago affair? Seems each time you bring it up, you slide back into depression. You deserve much better. Please, let it go!

Now that the Chicago incident is in the past, you must now refocus your attention on your assignments and seminars. I know it takes a lot of energy to focus when you have a nightmare weighing you down, but now that it is over, it is time to get the accumulated work done. I have all the confidence in you that what used to be an obstacle will now become an incentive and motivation for success. You make me nervous when you suggest that you are also considering a different degree program. I don't think this is a wise decision. How can you possibly complete the one you are working on now rapidly if you abandon it to start a new one? Instead of contemplating a new program, you should focus on the current one and complete it. It is not a smart thing to abandon a program half way. I would like to see you complete what you started. As for coming to visit you in the summer, I have already told you I will stay for one month. I have some classmates who work with travel agencies. Though they have bad attitudes and make fun of others, I am going to need them in order to secure a cheap ticket. They are already helping me see the best routes to take to get the best deals and discounts. I plan to purchase the ticket in May and process my passport between January and March. I would want you to help me secure an affordable summer class in English as a Second Language. I plan to arrive on a Saturday so that I do not interfere with your classes. I would also expect you to wait for me at the airport. Instead of taking a taxi, we can save some money by taking the bus from the airport. I love taking the bus since taxi drivers are usually dishonest. Just keep an open mind as I make my plans and you can orient me as we get closer to the dates. Before we move forward, we must resolve your unstable frame of mind. Don't you think? I am sure you are now feeling much better and looking forward to better things in life. I remember a postcard of yours describing the snow and cold weather. I found it very beautiful. If I were there with you, I would tell you about your bright eyes, shining like those of the fireflies. I wish I could just look into those penetrating eyes.

Let me reassure you that the worst times will soon pass for you and better times, days, and years are ahead. I love and adore you. You truly won my heart over. We were socialized not to tell any man that we love them as a woman. They say once a man knows that secret, he will no longer be interested. I think if this happens, such a man is ignorant. Such a man risks losing a jewel of his life upon whom to depend and enjoy an eternity full of happiness. Have confidence in me and in my sincerity. I pity those who take such feelings for granted. I pity them indeed. Even if I should die tomorrow, I would be at peace with myself for loving you until the end. Christmas is just around the corner and I am having such a wishful thinking that you might surprise us with your own visit. I know you are so unpredictable. Wouldn't that be nice? Well, should that happen, oh, I will wrap you around me and never let you go. But don't kill yourself. Enjoy your life, get your work done, get good grades, and do not allow any negative energy to change you as a person. I am sincerely missing you even as close as I am to you. When will this stage of deep feelings and desires stop? I will always be yours in a relationship that is pure and divine. We need to preserve this special love of ours, nurture it forever, and ensure that above all, there is mutual respect and consistent dialogue. As I mentioned before, I am feeling the burden of exams as I am in the midst of finals. In case my communication wanes, it has nothing to do with you. It is just that I must also focus on preparing for the exams ahead of me to complete the semester. In the meantime, I encourage you to remain your strong self, a good and loving man who must overcome his vulnerabilities through struggle and confidence. No room for laziness or excuses. You remind me of a Brazilian musician, Djavan who sings: "Meu bem querer / É segredo, é sagrado / Está sacramentando / Em meu coração"[2] [My love, my beloved, / it is a secret, it is sacred, / it is sacramented in my heart]. That is how I feel about our relationship. It is sacred. I am relieved. I am happy.

    Let me share a parable with you, an experience of overcoming the odds by a paraplegic man who wanted to climb a 5,000-meter mountain. The first time he tried, he fell and was hospitalized for 12 days. Yet, he did not give up because he was clear about his goal. After recuperating, he decided to try again after many exercises and physical therapies. He made it, despite the uncertainties. And you, with two legs and two arms, you are complaining about things you are unable to accomplish. Get out of your apathy and start moving towards your goal. Rise up into your destiny. Don't let your repulsion for the system overwhelm you. It is time to wake up from your slumber. Your path is open; all you need to do is attack the problem with all your energy and persevere to claim your victory. It is not easy for us black people. You have to be four times as good to make it in this white world. So start early, so that before you are 40 years old, you can at least claim victory. My own brother learnt that early in life, like when he was 12 or 14-years-old, about the hard life of blacks. He resolved to study philosophy and now as an adult, he will be publishing a book. It takes sacrifices to overcome the odds against us. So, we need to be active and resolved in our mission as a couple. It is not over until it is over. I remember returning to Liberdade, the Japanese community in São Paulo. I stopped by the same restaurant we had eaten together, *Restaurante Shangai*, before you left Brazil. It was raining at the restaurant the last time I was there. Though I went by myself, I felt your presence while I was there. I even dozed off while waiting for the food and thinking of you. By the

---

2   https://codes.findlaw.com/il/chapter-720-criminal-offenses/il-st-sect-720-5-12-3-05.html. Accessed July 28, 2018.

time the food came, I woke up and said to myself: "Only you can make me happy!"

As special as our communication is to my soul, its intensity overwhelms me so much that I wish I could resolve the distance issue and spend less time in contemplations and meditations. Our communication has gotten you hooked, like a drug, on someone across the Atlantic motivating you to be the best you can be. Were you not the leader of your group of students when I visited you in Butantã in 1982? So what happened to that same charismatic character? You called me recently. It was quite a moment. I was able to express myself better. I could also feel your voice and know that you are fine. Yet, you make me ask questions over and over due to the reality of the distance between us. I do find a purpose in all of this. You make me feel like a counselor, but in fact, I just love you as you are. One thing I recognize in you and am trying to figure out is the reason you think so deeply and so much? There is a difference between thinking about solutions to problems and actually taking steps to solve those challenges. On the one hand, you are avoiding getting your work done and on the other, you justify that laziness by reflecting on issues that overwhelm you. I think that you have identified the issues blocking you and you can begin to address the constraints, and set an agenda of priorities that will help you redirect your energies and take action. This action will counter the lethargy that I think you are suffering at the moment. Even when you hypothetically establish that the people around you are fake, racist, competitive, unfriendly, indifferent, cold, and even heartless, you must raise your mindset and rise above them, so that you can visualize a time in the future when they will come to pay homage to you because you are well beyond their pedestrian level. Let your adversaries be the least of your problem. What needs to happen is self-preservation. You need to rise to the occasion of unlimited possibilities. Don't be ashamed to take concrete steps towards what makes you happy. Ever since you were in Brasília, I have been hearing these complaints about accumulated work. Once you look into your inner self, discover your true vision despite the solitude, and you will tackle this progressive marasmus enveloping you. Accept that you have a different profession in mind because academic life is nothing but just this penchant you are resisting: read and read and read!

What exactly did you expect from an academic career? Did you expect it to be an adventure? You think you are on summer vacation? Do you consider yourself a tourist? Wake up, Clétus! Be determined and make sure you are eating well. You need a balanced diet to be strong and clear-sighted. I was reading an article not too long ago and discovered the connection between quality of life, academic stress, and sound health. I will find the article and see if I can send parts of it to you, but in the meantime, here is the summary: "…university students are deemed to suffer from a few psychosocial problems such as anxiety, low self-esteem, depression, relationship difficulties, stress, and excessive preoccupation with studies" (Cerchiari, 1987)[3]. If you can refocus your energy and balance different stressors by identifying the positive outcome in the process of sacrificing time and imagination, you will find out that it is all worthwhile if you learn to have a balance. You will notice that I have been trying to keep in touch with you with the same intensity that you have. While you have been more spontaneous, I have had to wait to accumulate your communication and respond to them over the weekend, which is the only time I have for myself. I wonder how your adaptation is going. Are you still under pressure to give up due to stress or are you more determined to persevere until you attain your objectives? I am sure you have taken the route of completing your degree. I think completing the degree in less time will be good for you

---

3   Phillippe Cerchiari, *Une île magnifique dans le Pacifique* (Paris: L'Harmattan, 2018).

and having such an accomplishment would set you apart as not many black people have that opportunity.

Given our passionate journey so far, and as you make the quantum leap in achieving your objective, I hope you bear in mind this black woman who loves you very much. What do you say? I know I occupy a good place in your heart, but one never knows with men. Our communication is so profound, and yet, I have no trust in this decadent world. We are living in a world that is mentally sick, without solidarity, respect, affection, or love. Thus, I am obliged to remind you that I want to always be by your side. I want to be so close and present in your life. We are already very close in our cosmic communication though I am not so sure how you will react to my expectations. I thank God for my feeling this way; it is so very beautiful and rare. You have contributed significantly to my feeling this way, making me more secure, confident, and hopeful of life. I often wonder how you were able to escape the brutality of this world and still remain sane, loving, caring and human. Why are you so different and affectionate? Why are you so sensitive, honest and philosophical? Do you exist for me to believe that God exists and there is hope after all? I wanted to share with you an outing we did as a family: my mom, the kids, my brother, and his girlfriend. It was a feast to celebrate the outing of Ogun and Obaluaiê saints or Orixás. I am sure you are familiar with Candomblé. We left home on Saturday evening and returned only on Sunday morning. There was food made for the deities. The following Monday, my classmates presented a drama sketch in honor of the Orphanage on Praça Roosevelt. It was an emotional presentation on the theme of "Ecology for Children." I was so emotional that I cried throughout the presentation. To end the day, I returned to that Japanese restaurant in Liberdade where we have gone together many times. It was as if you were there with me all the time. You brought back great memories. I can only imagine how all I do and say make you feel. Oh! Only you can make me happy...

Not only are the days feeling like months and months feeling like years since your departure, but the efforts to love each other from a distance is also taking its toll on both of us. As I try to cope with my anguish, the lyrics of Milton Nascimento come to mind to keep me company in his "Caçador de Mim"[4] (Hunter of Myself): "Prisoner to songs / Submissive to passions / That are endless / I will only find myself away from my location / I, hunter of myself... / Nothing to fear / But the flow of struggle / Nothing else to do / If not forget all fear." Nascimento captures my frame of mind as I wander through the nights for my absent lover and all I can be consoled with is music and the hope of rejoining my lover somewhere across the river. Frankly, I want to be by your side always. I could not be myself when you called me at the Institute because my colleagues were around—so I could not be myself. I wanted to actually scream with emotions but had to control myself. I want you to remain strong and not let the school work drain you. Do the best you can and know it is for the best. I just do not want you to give up no matter what. Recently, I had the privilege to watch on television physically challenged famous individuals who use their feet to paint after losing their hands to some unfortunate accident. I am sharing these items so that you can be determined to succeed no matter what. I also had an incident in 1981 when I fell off a motorcycle. My left knee was inflamed but after a series of painstaking efforts, a physician took my case and I was able to recover the use of my knee after two weeks of treatment. Most nurses had predicted that I was going to lose the use of my left leg. But today, I am a winner. I overcame the odds. In the same way, I have every confidence that you will succeed in the end despite the odds. Anita Baker's music, comes to soothe my spirit: "You

---

4 Milton Nascimento, *Caçador de Mim* (São Paulo: Universal Brazil, 2007).

bring me joy / Don't go too far away / If I can't see your face. I will / remember that smile ... / But can this be right / Or should we be friends / I get lonely sometimes and I'm / mixed up again / 'Cause you're the finest thing I've / seen in all my life / You bring me joy."[5] Instead of suffering, this is how I cope. Can you do the same and suffer less?

I now realize the extent to which Lúcia was invested in my success. Her approach was to negate nostalgia as a way to cope with past pain and agony. Two lives are intertwined by sheer providence despite distance and through cosmic communication that defies all human understanding. Through that negation of negation, nostalgia persists. Nostalgia need not be negative; but it must be properly channeled in order to make sense of a confusing impasse. I never understood the saying that someone enjoys suffering. If they could help their situation, I doubt if the one suffering would not want to change the situation. It is all a matter of perception.

---

5   Anita Baker, *Rhythm of Love* (New York: Rhino Atlantic, 1994).

8

Nostalgia Plus

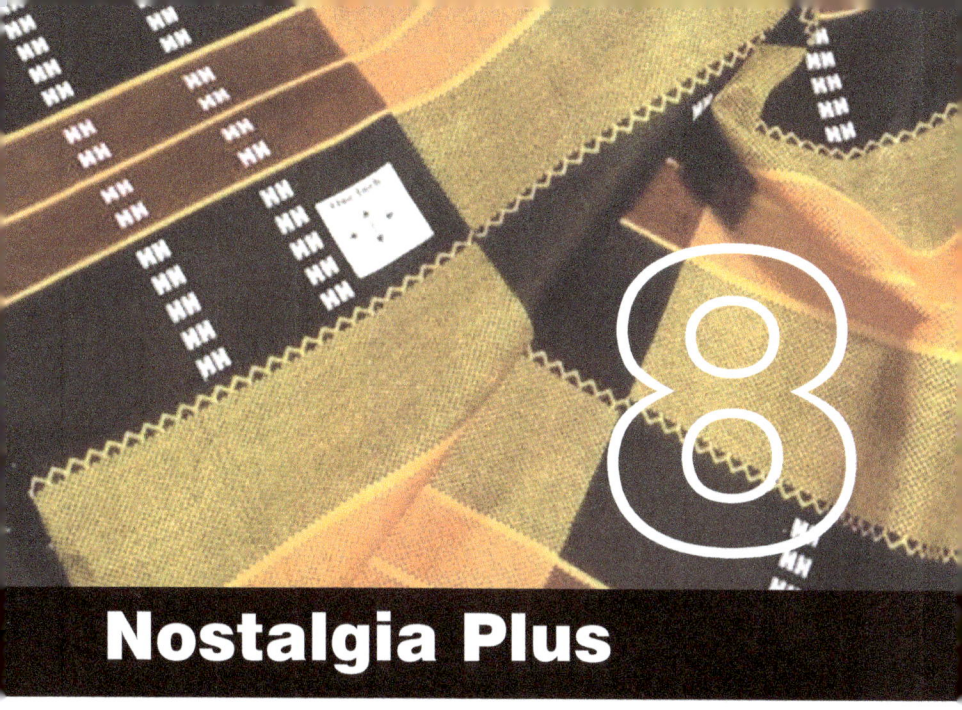

Aisha and Fayola
©Barbosa Archives 2018

Nostalgia manifests itself in different grades and shades. We often take the presence of loved ones for granted when we see them too frequently. There is also that unusual moment when we are away from them for a short while and we miss them very intensely. Yet, missing someone because of their goodness, affinity, or character is not the same thing as missing a loved one. The pain is not describable. It is as if a part of us is completely gone and nothing is ever the same. For lovers, it is like mourning when we miss each other. Lúcia and I have had our many years of shared nostalgia. We tried through communication to numb the nostalgia. The negation or denial of nostalgia does not mean it is no longer there. It is just that for some awkward reason, maybe even a mature sense of giving sense to nonsense, we have come to see the reality as inevitable. Notwithstanding, one gets a sense that in matters of the heart, nostalgia could be heightened through extended passage of time and it may be more appropriate to call it "nostalgia plus." Such was my feeling about the saga of the passionate journey between Lúcia and me over the decades. Whether it is during the day or during the night; whether at work or driving home; working on school assignments or contemplating a solution to daily challenges, nostalgia has become part of life. Indeed, given its long tenure among two people who love each other to the extreme, it has become a way of life, a solution to deep emotions and even melancholy. Nostalgia is the sane way of purging the mind of total insanity, a form of therapy that even specialists may find ingenious.

I, Lúcia, come in the name of Oxum [deity of the rivers] to reveal my profound anxieties. I harmonize my own soul in the process of stabilizing yours. We complement each other. I feel whole every time I am able to communicate with you from the deepest abyss. My Beloved, it is a little over midnight. I had thought my finals would affect the rhythm of our communication but love overpowered all the challenges and I am deploying my entire soul in the service of a tranquil sojourn close to your heart. I feel as if you were speaking into my ears, whispering, Lúcia, Lúcia, Lúcia! I am hearing this consistent call as if you were right beside me and we are rocking each other back and forth. I can see that you are successfully balancing your academic work, the stimulating force even if adversarial that your professor constitutes, the unbearable weather, and the culture shock that is taking its toll on every aspect of your being. I am happy and quite relieved. This is one more aspect of many lived experiences that must be stored up in your own archives of professional growth, as they constitute impetus for your reaching for a greater destiny. You are acquiring the basic tools of your professional trade that will allow you in the near future to navigate complex challenges with much facility. Consequently, you will ultimately be respected by everyone; and when I say "everyone" I mean by the very same people who currently constitute artificial barriers to your social uplift.

Since my last apparition, three issues have developed among others that require my response. One is your feeling the need to provide encouragement to me as well although you did not have any obligation to do so. I appreciate the positive energy you have sent me to keep going as well. I thought it was so beautiful and sensitive of you. I would love everything to remain as spontaneous as it has been to date. I believe this is how we will get to our desirable destination. Were you being philosophical when you wondered when we will arrive at our destination as lovers and a couple as opposed to the constant points of departure that seem to characterize our relationship for many decades? Life is full of these shifting stages and there will always be both working hand-in-hand until we create the ideal moment to make the impossible possible by getting married and living under the same roof. Kindly let me know if I made the point clear or if I need to be even more specific. I wonder if I shared my clippings on the coldness of some countries such as Germany. The naïve feature articles suggest that couples reluctantly have children but instead, adopt animals to keep them company. Alternatively, adopted children are often abused; while lonely elders offer to pay young students in order to converse with them. I wanted to know if the situation you are in is similar. All I am suggesting is that you become open to such possibilities of joining forces together so you can be a winner in all you do. I am not a bad person in any way. You cannot even imagine how much love and affection I reserve inside of me for you. I just hate to be made fun of later on that I invested in this or that someone else pushes me to a point where I give it all up out of frustration and thus hurt myself in the process.

Once again, I am still trying to rationalize my attitude towards you last year when you first arrived back in Brazil after many years in Nigeria. I was truly giving up on humanity then. Perhaps this is God's way of letting me have another chance at working out our so special feelings towards a concrete outcome.

Pardon me, Clétus. You raised issues about people's comportment that you were trying to understand. I shared my own experiences by referencing the comparative attitudes of humans, animals, dogs, and family. In essence, I was leading to the issue of marriage. For me, to get married is to become one with another person, to be in perpetual harmony without offense, aggressive arguments, belittling each other. Rather, marriage should always be encouraging, advising, and celebrating each other through dialogue. I see no other form of happiness towards professional success that transcends this search for equilibrium between couple. As I listen to blues, I feel like embracing you, remembering the program "Black in love," and wishing I could share your solitude and other experiences with you so that it all becomes more bearable for you. It is a pity that seniors are discriminated against in many societies. They have so much to offer in terms of helping by offering their inestimable experience to many people in crisis. You also tend to treat me as a special person, by comparing me to the American woman in the elevator who jokingly gave you two little kisses and said no third one because three is for those who want to marry. I found it very funny and I am flattered. You know what, I am not that different from you. Perhaps we just have this sensibility that makes us special. I am truly sorry for all you are going through so far away from me but soon enough, we will be together.

Frankly, I don't feel any differently from the way you feel; I just think I am suffering from your elusive warmth as well. Perhaps over the years, I have been able to absorb many activities through which I suppress and hide from myself my lack of special love and warmth. The need to have someone speak with the same tone, same sensibility, to the extent that I feel so special when you call me "beloved." Whenever I hear you ask: "Are you ok? Do you need help? Courage! Everything is going to be alright!," I feel so specially loved. As a result, it is very easy for me to return the warmth back to you as someone who truly deserves my care and affection. In a way, what I expect others to do for me, the way I want to be treated, that is exactly what I pass on to you in a special way. I cannot afford to be weak when someone like you by my side is weak. It feels so good to love you. So good. My brother is making posters in preparation for the launching of his novel, *Paixões Crioulas*[1] [Creole Passions] while my sister and I are working on a feast, "Uma Noite em África" [A Night in Africa], to be held at the school of samba, *mocidade alegre* [Happy Youth], near our house. Pardon me for all the passionate words I shared the last time. I had to get it all out. I did not mean to overwhelm you. The words just came and I felt like sharing them to feel closer to you. I could not help myself because I feel as if we were just having a normal conversation side by side through that magical communication. I think this is the only way we can truly get to know each other better. Perhaps I am special and different only because no one is the same. I can be very strong when the situation warrants it. The feast went well; I returned home

---

[1] Márcio Barbosa, *Paixões Crioulas* (São Paulo: Quilombhoje, 1987).

and washed my car, clothes, and prepared for an intense week ahead. My boss at the Institute will be leaving for Washington D.C. and needs me to prepare some documents to take with him. It is so difficult for me to let it pass but I feel that you should be here with me to go to all these feasts and events. I would like you to share my happy and sad moments as well. At times, I ask myself if it makes sense for us to be so far away from each other especially when our quest for our well-being is mutual.

There is something I have always wanted to ask you. You mentioned that you fast occasionally. I would like you to be careful about this. We can only absorb rational principles and not religious indoctrinations that can harm us. Do avoid fanatical ideologies that mask themselves as ministers and pastors asking for money. Just a brief thought and caution that I want to share with you. If you ever need to have any spiritual guidance, make sure it is with a balanced and intelligent person. Not a religious fanatic. This past weekend I slept a lot because I was menstruating. I felt as if I slept all weekend long. I am very much in love with you. I want to make love to you all the time. There are a lot of things I want to tell you. I want to tell you that I truly love you. I am also afraid you may turn around and lose interest in me for saying what I feel naturally. Anyway, must be thoughts from past relationships. I look forward to being together, have a son or daughter as well as a dog to protect us, no one to replace our love but to protect the family. I am sure you are saying to yourself: "This lady only thinks about having a child." Well, it is a beautiful thing, especially if it was conceived in love. I am overwhelmed by many thoughts and I must share them with you. You are a very special being; you give me so much attention the same way I give you so much attention. I also have the audacity to say that everything is real and one day we shall be living together in Brazil. Is this too much to ask for and desire?

How nice of you to have called me. Goodness! A phone call from Clétus? What a limitless expression of joy and so much emotion. The emotion was such that all of a sudden I found it difficult to express myself. All I could do was to observe as the words suffocated in my throat, with happiness and pleasure, all at the same time. An expression of love and a sensation of love to speak with you. After the brief conversation, I started wondering why we really met, the mystery of the encounter, an African from so far away. Tell me, what is ahead for us, tell me! Well, no point for me to be so anxious, wanting to foretell the future. I must be patient and persist until time, destiny, and God tell us what the purpose of our initial encounter is. What exactly is the meaning of this relationship? Even this singular communication of ours, this passionate aura, and luck, I have never felt like this in many years, nor could I believe something like this to be possible. It is as if I spoke with you for the first time in a dream. It is like a dream indeed to be able to communicate with you; and for you to be a person who loves to communicate. Being with you is like flying, dancing, and dreaming infinitely.

It is a great thing to love each other. We love each other selflessly. It has nothing to do with egoism. To love each other is to look into one another's face, embrace each other, enjoy each other, and transfer all the love to the one who deserves it and who also loves us. On the contrary, egoism is about loving the other to get attention, while not giving anything in return. This act of selfishness is not healthy and it is bad. A little bit of pride is good but not a whole lot. But why I am saying all this? Who knows, my beloved? All of my classmates and I are having a challenging time. We are in the peak moment of finals. We are basically crying on each other's shoulder. We need each other's support with so much to prepare and present for finals. I must now sleep. I am exhausted. I hope you are enjoying this communication and I look forward to your responses. Feel free to talk about whatever you want. In the meantime, we are entering the month of December and Christmas is beckoning. You are such a special person because your sensibility extrapolates that of any individual on this planet. You are able to respond to stimuli due to your sensitivity. When it comes to stress, we all use vitamins and you should not be left out. As for my complaints about feeling abandoned due to loneliness, it was just a ploy for you to keep communicating. I receive at least four letters from you every week. That is a lot. I am sorry for telephoning so early the other day. You renew my energies by your caring demeanor. I am feeling tired and sleepy. I am also in the second week of finals. The body needs to rest a little, however little.

Unfortunately, I am unable to sleep. I feel like embracing you now, kissing you wildly, and looking deeply into your eyes, like a wave of eccentric love that deafens, even blinds, and all we can hear is the heartbeat as we feel our lips on top of each other's lips, the bodies touching closely in an intimately integrated tango. Only entering into one another's inner chambers do we complete each other in a journey that is completely transcendental and cosmic. And for a few moments of passionate escapades we are no longer on this planet earth. As we switch confused movements from one space to another, we gradually find ourselves at a higher plane that is completely different from where we were before taking off from this earth. By the time we realize the fullness of the strange moment, what transpired is so magical to both of us, as well as to those who see kaleidoscopic mysteries in our absorbing eyes right after. Where was I all this while? Where were you my love? Where were we? The riveting mood can only be soothed through the spontaneous manifestation of melodies. Maria Bethânia comes to my rescue when she sings to me: "I am feeling nostalgic of you my desire / It is so difficult to be without you / Your odor gives me pleasure / My thought travels uninhibited / And I go in search of my beloved / Nostalgia of embrace ... of kisses / With you I find myself in the arms of peace ... / Nostalgia ... of your affectionate gaze."[2] I am so out of control; but somehow, I was able to sleep as the night took over what was left of my serenated body. By the time I woke up it was the dawn of a new day. Oh! What a magical journey of love! I am ready for a new day indeed.

For some reason I cannot explain to myself, I am deeply missing you. I thought of calling you but I also worry you may not be at home and finding out that I called you may make you nervous. I wonder where you are now and what you are doing. I wonder if you are able to interpret this our moment of sheer profundity. I hope you are still taking your vitamins for stress? I want to believe you are coping better with your school work and your possible visit in December or January. You never talk about your family or ethnic group. Is it true that young girls are already promised to men from birth or is that just one of the stereotypical beliefs about Africa? I am sure you will respond when you are less busy. How do I deal with this incredible nostalgia? Perhaps this will all be taken care of when I visit you in July. I will have to wait all this time to embrace you and kiss you? What a difficult man you are! My exam today is on Law. Yesterday's exam was on Accountancy. The last exam will be on Marketing. I want to repeat my request for you to eat well and take vitamins so you can have a balanced health. Avoid any form of fasting. You can reduce your food intake but never become hooked on fasting. It is not good for your system. You can end up in a medical coma. You often ask if I am lonely. Of course, I am lonely even amidst pretenders that I run from. I run from them because they do not have your qualities. Once they manage to get a taste of the only thing they want, soon enough, they are nowhere to be found, ever again.

---

2   Maria Bethânia, *Gostoso Demais* (São Paulo: Celluloid, 1988).

That is not what I want. I want you. I need you. Only you can make me happy.

You must wonder why time has become my closest friend instead of an enemy. I guess we create time when we are foolishly in love. With an endless flow of communication back and forth, in the midst of work, school, and family, you must begin to wonder if I am not losing my mind. If my actions are read as madness, then I would rather be insane for a genuine love than lose this unique moment of renewal. I am truly not ashamed to be happy in the arms of my loved one. I am suddenly transported by Almeida Garrett's *Viagens na Minha Terra* [Travels in My Land] to a pastoral valley where he describes the source of inspiration to his creative sensibilities: "O vale de Santarém é um destes lugares privilegiados pela Natureza... Se haverá ali quem aproveite a deliciosa janela?... Se for homem é poeta; se é mulher está namorada. São os dois entes mais parecidos da Natureza, o poeta e a mulher namorada; vêem, sentem, pensam, falam como a outra gente não vê, não sente, não pensa nem fala"[3] [The Santarém valley is one of these places privileged by Nature ... Could there be someone there who enjoys the delicious view? ... If it is a man, he is a poet; If it is a woman, she is in love. They are the two most similar beings of Nature, the poet and the woman in love; they see, they feel, they think, they speak like other people do not see, do not feel, do not think or speak]. I have become the traveler of the soul, body, and spirit, all in the quest for my beloved Clétus. I would not trade anyone for him. I see in him the "poet" while I am the "woman in love" that Garrett references. United we are in the act and name of love. Your phone call was a blessing. It reinvigorated my desire to embrace you so close to me, squeeze you in love even for a few moments. Pity you are so far away from me in this chaotic world that I traverse every day. Only you can make me happy.

---

3   Almeida Garrett, *Viagens Na Minha Terra* (Lisboa: Clássicos, 2004).

Just when I was having a blast in your love and mine, the flashes of the past came to haunt me especially concerning the Chicago affair. I probably would not have been bothered but seems you reacted to my jealous curiosities in terms of wanting to know more... You decided to speak in parables; perhaps out of pain and shock; not wanting to give details... I was left wondering and conjecturing that maybe you had done something for the young girl to have reacted so mean-spiritedly or naively... Just because you did not give me any concrete detail to go by. It was thus very painful for me to be reading your communication between the lines and sensed that my words had hurt you and you felt that I did not trust you. You felt betrayed by your special love. So let's return to the issue for clarification. Since you were not ready to give details, I had to make something up. I knew you to be a conversationalist. So I felt, maybe you were trying to have a conversation with the poor girl and she rejected your advances. I am not saying that was what happened. I am just making things up in my head in order to make sense of this horror story. I share your pain as well. I wished nothing of this nature had happened to you. I am very sorry I caused you pain in addition to the pain of injustice you experienced in Chicago. Will you forgive me? I know you have a transcendental spirit and you have forgiven me. I just could not help myself. I felt that you were befriending the girl somehow. It was out of jealousy on my part that I reached that conclusion and it was not that I did not trust or was making your situation worse. We feel pain when wrongly accused and for the one we love to be questioning us on the matter makes matters worse, I understand. Please forgive me once again. I cried knowing that I caused you pain, but now we both know why. It was just silly jealousy on my part! Nothing more.

Your puzzling question if I was pregnant blew me away. It was just out of character... Not expected at all. Something we never discussed. You know, for some days and moments, I felt that you were asking this question. I am not even sure why I had such flashes that such questions were going through your mind. My answer to your question is that as long as we are in an unsettled situation, it would be bad for the child. Clétus, my darling; today, I suffer from a terrible experience of which I am even ashamed. I hardly discuss this with anyone except close relatives. I have to raise my son all by myself, without the love of his father. It is a selfish undertaking for us to bring a child into the world without a collective plan on how to raise him and give him love. Perhaps you will be an exception to the rule of men who run away from their responsibility. Honestly, I suffer the same way Sandro suffers for lacking the presence of his dad in his life. It makes me very sad. And talking about sadness, it is not just about being responsible for the schooling of the child; it is not just even about money; it touches issues of ethics, spiritual well-being, moral standards, having a male role model in his life, building character, setting objectives, and learning to be a man through guidance and examples... You know what all that entails. Sincerely, I would like the father of my next child to be living with me as a couple. Look, you have really asked a great question. Now, you have given the opportunity to bare my heart on the matter. You may have forgotten; I think you were in Brasília then, I was asking you to be the father of my child; it was just a spontaneous wish then. My darling, to answer your question, no, I am not pregnant. If I were, I would have told you. Why hide something so beautiful? And let me ask you what would you have done about it? Finally, let's leave the Chicago affair behind us. As for coming to visit you in July, let's hope for the best. The plan is to come to take a summer class in English and if my finances are not able to cover it and yours also not enough to sustain yourself, then we just have to defer it to another time. For now, I am staying positive on the agreement that I will see you in July.

8 - Nostalgia Plus

 Faced with your reaction to my questioning of the Chicago affair and wishing you can forgive and forget that episode or any attitude or reaction to it, let me now flow freely with you on many issues and hope that you will make the effort to respond when you have a chance. We both have so much in common. You have come to reassure me that this world still has someone I can put my trust in and with whom I can possibly build a future. You came into my life at a time I was ready to give up on human beings in general, especially in love. The world seems to consider as stupid those individuals who have pure feelings, sensibility, love, warmth to give away but without finding the right person. On the contrary, the world that deceives us and sees us as ignorant is in fact stupid when we process things from the viewpoint of spirituality. I would like to know more about your daily activities beyond teaching. Be not offended, darling, of my numerous questions. It is just my way of coping with missing you so much and having the need to chat with you on many things. I do not mean to invade your privacy with so many questions, I am just curious. I am also curious that the church you are attending is not exercising any form of brain washing on you. You need to believe in yourself and not let anyone control your mind. Before I sleep every night, I try to transmit to you protective energy from the Infinite Energy. Just to touch on the airplane event again: I am sure it was just a misunderstanding between the two of you. I am sorry for appearing to be judging you; that was not my intention. Perhaps you should learn to keep to yourself more and talk less with everyone. Human beings are not spiritually mature and you just have to develop your own consciousness to the highest level possible. You will gradually feel much better and in control of your life.

 I know when it comes to spiritual matters, you may think I am exaggerating when I say religious people tend to be fanatical and you have to be careful about those with whom you mingle.

Be sure you know yourself and do not fall a victim of religious ideologies. If you do not appear weak or helpless, no one will dare to take undue advantage of you spiritually. I miss you so much and cannot wait to see you again. As I hear the songs of the night birds, I can only imagine how it would be as we get older, to see if we can travel across the oceans to see each other. Maybe there is a way you can get here, too, via astral traveling. My wishful thinking again! Despite my confused thoughts, the music of Maria Bethânia soothes my spirit once again even as I am beginning to feel sleepy. Please, do find the time to reply to my tons of questions and curiosities. Caetano Veloso is also singing to me: "Soy louco por ti America"[4] (I am crazy about you America]. That makes the two of us who are crazy about Brazil and the Americas. It is a good feeling. You hardly talk about your students though I understand if you are busy and do not want to dwell into details of their behavior. I just hope you are heeding the advice of taking daily vitamins for stress. Though I am studying Tourism Management, I wish I could be a teacher someday. The more I appreciate our relationship, as an Afro-Brazilian woman, with a jet black African color as if I am from Nigeria like you, I also lament the confused ideology of miscegenation in Brazil that makes black people feel so strangely ashamed of their blackness. Instead of marrying fellow Afro-Brazilians, they would rather marry white women to feel secure. This makes me so furious about back people being ashamed of their color. Worse still is the influence of the social media as young ones are overwhelmed with urban violence through films and cartoons. I urge you, now that our relationship is getting better and better, to not interrupt the rhythm of our cosmic communication that has become my unique sustaining energy.

---

[4] Caetano Veloso, "Soy Loco Por Ti América," https://www.letras.mus.br/caetano-veloso/76612/. Accessed August 5, 2018.

By their sheer prophetic power of pronouncement, these spontaneities of the soul will serve as a historical document one day. Today, they function as frames of mind as one soul communicates with the other across the Atlantic; tomorrow, they become the fulfillment of revelation. This is your birthday anniversary month. I declare that by the time I complete this manifestation of memory, all that has been ordained for your glory will become expressly manifest. I activate the purpose of your life by the transformative power of the word. As usual, I am addressing the issues summarily—from unfinished issues between us, through encouraging you towards fulfillment of your destiny, to my own curiosities that are often triggered by nostalgia. I just cannot help myself in wanting to know what and how you are doing in view of our protracted distance. I still feel privileged and it is as if I am in a kind of dream-like state of mind. You cannot possibly exist as a human being due to your compassion and dedication. When I contemplate you, the precise words do not come to help me communicate exactly how I feel about you. While at work, I read a few things in the news concerning increases in child prostitution in Brazil and in the USA. Human beings think by having sex they will be more relaxed but the contrary is the case; they are deceiving themselves; rather, they become addicted and violent. In order to become relaxed, there is need for love. I think having sex is best when there is no anxiety about ejaculation. Imagine having sex in love, just one lover inside the other, loving and transcending their immediate space. I am awaiting my bus and it is taking too long. You remember my school right? We had gone there together once. It was that year I refused to be with you; I was not ready to fool myself and suffer. But it did not help running from you. You have become my destiny.

When I arrived home, I quickly found something to eat but my mom came to tell me something concerning my dad. In the process, I was reading your letters and responding and she got into my business asking if you were receiving my letters. I told her not quite but that we have decided that you will come to visit in January and I will go there in July. She quickly jumped at the idea and said: "I will need to prepare an extra room and make things homely for him; otherwise, what will he think about us?" It made me feel good that my mother was supportive of our relationship. She even added: "Why does he not return to Brazil once and for all, and feel at home here? I would not stay over there for even a year. What if the white people kill him out of jealousy?" We left the matter at that. She is suggesting that you will be happier in Brazil and I agree with her. Ironically, Brazil is entering into an economic recession. Everything is rising in price such as gasoline, school fees, and food items. I could not even pay my rent this month; I have to wait until next month to pay it with interest. I am feeling some inner sadness and would like to ask if you are doing well and if our relationship is fine. While my brother received a letter from you, I did not receive any. This makes me wonder if you are angry with me because I am asking too many questions about your life and future plans. On another note, we are going through a situation at work. A white lady who does not do her work well or who is not well trained to do her work is being kept instead of being let go as we had concluded. The boss told us to help her out whenever she could not get her work done. Can you imagine? Do you see now that racial discrimination is everywhere? The boss wants us black women to do the work of a white woman whenever she is unable to complete her duties? That made me so mad. I need to hear from you now. Even if I have upset you by my words, please, communicate with me. Our communication is so natural; it must not stop. Let us preserve the jewel that God has given us for posterity.

    I am hoping that my returning to past issues is not considered as repetitive. I miss you so much and I am compelled to figure out a way to connect with you by any means necessary. The issues have ranged from your accumulated work, my doubts about the Chicago affair, your new adaptation efforts, and what appears to be a functional block due to lack of psychological support or the effects of nostalgia on your state of mind. I am crying right now because I wish you were right here with me. Is it possible for you to come for the holidays in December or January? That would truly console me a great deal. I am beginning to wonder if all of these marvelous emotions are just for a short while or if they are permanent. I am crying very profusely and profoundly. I guess, like you, I have to face the reality of solitude. You are adapting to attain your professional goals, what is the purpose of my own emotional suffering? I can see you returning to Brazil victorious, but it is taking too long. I send you positive energy especially in this special month of yours. It is an irony that my whole family went to the Independence Party of Nigeria and there were many Nigerians there and cultural activities as well, while you are over there lonely and melancholic. I want you to seriously consider the possibility of visiting us for Christmas, even if it is for a week or two. Imagine what it would be like for you to be among people who love you into the New Year? I am sure you will be very renewed and ready to face the next stages of the challenges of your degree program. I understand if it is impossible for now, but I am letting you know my feelings so that you can feel my pain too. I just try to put myself in your position and I doubt if I would be able to cope over there. You are very strong and you should be commended for all the hardship you have overcome. The best is ahead of you. What is past is past. The future that awaits you now is prosperous, more fulfilling than the obstacles that tried to stop you in the course of your spiritual and professional journey. You are a winner; you have nothing to fear. Only you can make me happy…

  Lúcia's fantastic return to share more spontaneities was quite consoling. She has been able to mix the negation of nostalgia with renewed energy of nostalgia as if she is in a state of confusion or dementia. On the one hand, I am being encouraged to face the odds and achieve my defined goals despite the challenges. On the other hand, she is double speaking by playing both sides. She is unable to help herself because my absence is making it difficult for her to function. I feel a sense of pressure to return to Brazil, if even for a short visit. Financially, the dream is elusive. The funds are not there but with her constant pressure, I wonder if I can really make her happy if I cannot raise the funds. I am hoping for the best but it does appear that nostalgia is a catalyst for mysteries and fantasies.

Season of Samba

Maria Bethânia.
©Barbosa Archives 2000

In conjuring the passage of life itself as a "season" or a slice of life, I am invoking the "season of samba" as a moment of reflection mixed with joyfulness and sadness. Samba is a lively rhythmical dance of Afro-Brazilian origin that has

155

evolved in Brazil over the years. No other feeling can transport one away from the immediate ambience of Salvador-Bahia to the arms of one's loved one than the lyrics of the samba of Maria Bethânia when she romantically evokes the impact of longing on the soul of a lover, especially in her famed track, "Sonho Meu"[1] [My Dream]: "My dream, my dream; / Will go in search of someone living far away / My dream / Will show this longing / My dream / With all its freedom / My dream / In my sky the guiding star is lost / The cold dawn only brings me sadness / My dream." It is a slow-paced romantic yet pulsating music, that arrests everything rational, while taking over the body in a balanced shaking of the feet and body. Such is the mixed sadness and joy that the enchanting rhythms of samba evoke. Though that was not my first samba, each time I listened to anyone, it brings back memories. The memory of Lúcia often triggers two things: samba and carnival. Though we never actually enjoyed carnival together, I know her to be an enthusiast as her entire family are visible members of the *mocidade alegre* school of samba in São Paulo. It was not only while in Salvador or São Paulo that these emotions return, but each time I land in Brazil or think of Brazil. Yet, samba has a lot of cultural history to it. It is a blend of African and European cultural heritage since the 1500s. Considered one of the popular dances from South America, it has emerged as part of Brazilian cultural identity. Introduced to Brazilian culture by African people who were enslaved in Brazil in the 19th century, it is rich in African beats coupled with a few influences from Latin America. Due to the attitude of European colonizers and upper-class Brazilians who considered the song and dance as "obscene," it was only after the abolition of slavery in 1888 that samba gradually gained in popularity, especially during the roaring 1920s.

---

1   Maria Bethânia, "Sonho Meu," *Álibi* (São Paulo: Universal Music Ltd, 1978).

Following the popularity of samba, particularly in Rio de Janeiro, the song and dance soon found its way into other parts of Latin America and to the rest of the world. Given its vibrancy and performative appeal, it was not long for it to create many forms in different settings of the favelas, dance halls, and ballrooms with varieties such as *Samba Gafieira* (influenced by Waltz and Tango, it is a partner dance); *Samba no pé* (solo dance, 2/4 rhythm with three steps as necessary); *Samba Axé* (solo dance; performed to slow or fast beats); *Samba Pagode* (typical of São Paulo and Rio de Janiero, intimate and of slow tempo); *Samba de roda* (a celebratory event that incorporates samba music, choreography and poetry; participants join the dance and observe as well as imitate; choreography is often spontaneous, based on movements of the feet, legs and hips), *Samba rock* (is influenced by rock music but with basic samba rhythm); and *Samba Reggae* (typical of Bahia and most popular samba style with Jamaican influence). Interpreters of samba are many, including Carmen Miranda, Pixinguinha, Caetano Veloso, Gilberto Gil, Maria Bethânia, Beth Carvalho, Ivan Lins, Alcione, Martinho da Vila, Elza Soares, Sandra de Sá, Zeca Pagodinho, Leci Brandão, Neguinho de Samba, and Neguinho da Beija-Flor, among others. As a symbol of national identity, samba has its regional and national diversity. Transcending race and class, it continues to serve as a unifying factor in Brazilian culture. It also features as a vital element of the luxurious carnival performance in Rio de Janeiro. Overall, the syncopated and rich rhythm of samba often translates as black resistance against cultural assimilation as well as an expression of freedom and identity for the underprivileged class.

I have chosen the theme of "samba" as an expression of the connection between Lúcia and I; an expression of love, nostalgia, and deep meditations. While samba evokes gyrating hip movements (called *umbigada*) with roots going back to the colonial period, it gained importance with a number of influences, from *maxixe*, *marcha*, *habanera*, and *polka*. It was ultimately re-arranged and refined by Pixinguinha (Alfredo da Rocha Vianna). Beginning in the 1930s, samba evolved as a subgenre known as samba-canção, which privileged melody over rhythm, sentimentalism over exuberance. By the 1950s, *samba-canção* lost its sentimental appeal to a funkier style of samba known as *samba-de-batucada* (using polyrhythmic sounds of multiple percussion instruments), which then became the heartbeat sound of most Afro-Brazilian *escolas de samba* (samba schools). By the 1970s, samba grew into a popular genre within MPB (música popular Brasileira [Brazilian Popular Music]) as exemplified by Milton Nascimento, Djavan and Ivan Lins, who modernized the traditional *batucada* style of samba by fusing it with rock, jazz and other popular musical forms. Magically, samba has been so transformed and popularized that it has become a common heritage for all Brazilians regardless of race and class. The Afro-Brazilian movement through the Afro-Carnival groups such as, Olodum and Muzenza injected samba-reggae into the musical mainstream of Bahian music as well as into the international frame of *Axé music*. I cannot see any other cultural expression that connects me with Brazil than samba and carnival. I owe it all to meeting Lúcia in Brazil for the first time in 1982.

Lúcia introduced me musically to a number of samba producers such as Martinho da Vila, Alcione, and Maria Bethânia when we first met in São Paulo and through our cosmic communication. Her meditative personality calls for music as the language of mysticism and as a coping mechanism with the oddities of life. For my research, early in my career, she took me to *Vai-Vai*, a school of samba that became part of my undergraduate thesis. This was all part of my season of samba. Even when I was no longer in Brazil, she ensured that materials on samba and carnival reached me in Nigeria and Brazil. There is something quite dedicated in her disposition towards me; and that generous gesture can never be easily forgotten. Samba and carnival have become iconic symbols of Brazilian hybridity despite elements of resistance in a few social movements that do not live only for daily or annual rituals of samba and carnival, especially in Bahia. The cultural manifestation of hybridity differs from *mestiçagem*, because the former is less of an hegemonic penchant towards dominant national identity. Rather, *mestiçagem* celebrates samba and other Afro-Brazilian cultural forms as symbols of "Brazilianness" and racial democracy to the point of rallying round different races to invest in a performance of shifting citizenship. One can argue that the political use of culture was initiated by President Vargas's appropriation of marginal performances as projects of modernity. Yet, Afro-Brazilian cultural producers of samba and carnival contest performances that claim "racial democracy," by pointing out their marginalizing possibilities, especially when controlled by white elites in Rio de Janeiro and São Paulo. Theoretically, hybridity permits Afro-Brazilians to negotiate power and political participation. Despite the efforts of the Vargas regime to modernize Brazil, the appropriated regional cultural forms such as samba, carnival and capoeira, did not improve the living conditions of Afro-Brazilians or their political participation. Though Brazilian cultural identity is favored against contradictory racial or ethnic divisions. As a result, Afro-Brazilian movements are compelled to challenge racism and authoritarianism. Whether contradictory or not, hybridity serves as the unifying dynamic to bring Afro-Brazilian cultural groups and mainstream Euro-Brazilians together in the celebration of samba and carnival for the whole population. I wish Lúcia could visit again. Season of samba is incomplete without her mysteries.

I, Lúcia, come in the name of Exu (crossroads deity) and Obatala (creation deity) to resolve the crossroads and the complexities of creation that have been the challenges of your restless being. We have been communicating about the coming of carnival and you have been asking me many questions. I decided to "visit" you to have a closer encounter and have some peace of mind as we dialogue on general issues, including samba and carnival. I have attached copious pages from *Veja* (January 27, 1988) that include a series of articles on the Brazilian economy as well as an interview with Gilberto Gil on Brazilian racism that I plan to send to you in the mail. Due to a holiday next week, we have a reduced workweek. The cultural director in the office went to Cuba and left me a lot of work to complete for her. I have a head-tie around my head because I put some cream on my hair to make it shiny and soft. I am writing while my brother is reading a lot, while listening to James Brown. I forgot the exact title of the Shakespearean play he is reading. This past weekend, I wish you were here. It was marvelous. We all wished you were here. We all think of you (my sister and I). We went to the rehearsal of the school of samba, *Camisa Verde e Branca* on Friday. On Saturday, I went to the swimming pool with Sandro by the clock on the USP campus. On Sunday, we went to the Chopp Feast (beer) during the rehearsal at *Camisa Verde*. We were there from 10PM until 4AM. It was fantastic, very much so. Oh Clétus, you would need to be back vibrating with us in 1989. One of the most emotional moments for me was when a paraplegic, aided by walking sticks climbed onto the stage and sang the samba of his school of samba. Oh what a lesson of life to learn! What a blessing to be alive and able to walk unaided. At times, I am saddened when young girls tell me I am short and fat. I have to pay attention to my weight by avoiding cravings. Oh Clétus, we are so normal and yet we are so dissatisfied.

    The samba pamphlet (lyrics by Roberto da Tijuca et al.) we were given while at *Mocidade Alegre* was dedicated to Paulo Vanzolini, a USP Professor and Director of the Museum of Zoology. During the rehearsal, all I could think of was you, your blackness, sensibility, and love. When you phoned me recently, your voice was trembling due to the cold. I became very sad and worried. What can I do to share my warmth and love with you? That is probably why I decided to visit you mysteriously. Let us read the lyrics of this samba together. It pays homage to Paulo Vanzolini, tracing his trajectory as a scientist but who also loves samba: "What a marvel, the poet-scientist / Paulo Vanzolini in the inner chamber of poetry / ... / God bless you, your works / I will never forget / ... / Oh how nostalgic I feel / Enter the circle I want to see you dance samba." As we read this samba together, I observe that the person being honored has something in common with you. You may not be a scientist, but you are a poet. You are also a creative scientist by the organized way you like to get things done. You are very precise, organized, and scientific in a way. Whenever we speak on the phone, I always wished you were close. Since you kept asking about carnival, I wonder why you could not come now and forget suffering with reading novels of 800 pages. You folks read so many books but remain so inexperienced about life. I am afraid that after so many years of reading you may become contaminated and lose your ability to love. It is a paradox that the more people study, the more they become ignorant about real life. I just want to be alone with you, so that quietly, we can transmit feelings, words, and responses using our bodies to communicate. I am going to apply for my passport. I am resolved to go and see you. My Director at the Institute is putting so much trust in me; as a result, I am compelled to work four times harder, so as not to have any mistake whatsoever. In the whole of the University of São Paulo system, I do not know of any Administrative Executive working for a Director who is a black woman. I will surely see you soon and we will not only see each other, we will also feel each other. Everything is going to be fine, by God's grace.

Let me reassure you that until I eventually travel to the USA, I will keep the dreams of going to see you alive so that I can feel the warmth of your body. Now that carnival is over, let me share some of the memories with you. In São Paulo, *Vai-Vai* won the first place. In Rio de Janeiro, *Vila Isabel*, the school of samba, whose president is the famed musician you know, Martinho da Vila, was the winner. In our own local school of samba, *Camisa Verde e Branca*, a group of Angolans paraded but they could not celebrate due to heavy torrential rains that ended killing thousands of people. I pray that everything is fine with you. I worked at the Institute on Saturday and Sunday. My classes will start soon after carnival and things will get more stressful. I thought of phoning you, but decided to wait a while as I wondered: "Why should I be the one calling all the time?" Now let us read the samba lyrics of the *Vai-Vai* school that won in this year's carnival. Written by Oswaldinho da Cuica, Namur, and Macalé do Cavaco, and with the theme of Bahia, it celebrated the magic of the city and the works of the famed writer, Jorge Amado, as well as the presence of Afro-Brazilian religion. Beyond the general characteristics of Bahia, the centrality of miscegenation was also highlighted: "Bahia / Your name starts / With songs and magic / That blacks do breathe into the air. /… / Your past and present / Your future only God can tell." As we analyze this samba together, you see that you know some part of Brazil better than most Brazilians. I have never been to Bahia but you have lived in Bahia as part of your cultural immersion in my country and now you are in the USA. This is the privilege you have as an educated man. I cannot wait to behold and embrace you, love you like never before. I miss you, my darling.

 I often arrive home as late as 8PM. It has been like that for two consecutive days, after long hours of arduous work. I brought Sandro home with the intention of returning to school… complete deception… I could not even get off my seat due to tiredness. I quickly ate corn... all to no avail. I did not make it. I just simply could not make it. My consolation was seeing your beautiful mail waiting for me. I was so very overjoyed. For days, I had been avoiding feeling melancholic and losing hope about receiving your missive like before, for not receiving any of your communication. Your letter set out by addressing the academic rhythm that explained your lack of time and how you felt like you were losing your mind. You felt the system has a penchant for lies and masking. I must say that I appreciate it when you call me "beloved" and "darling." As for your conflicts regarding the system, the people, and culture, I think it is a great admission of the reality but it is always dangerous. Thanks to God, you are very similar to me in many ways, especially when it comes to sensibility and suffering. However, when we suffer a lot or find ourselves in certain circumstances that push us to the limit, we are forced to see no other solution but to withdraw within ourselves in order to not reveal our pain and suffering. We often need to swallow ourselves up, swallow the pain as if nothing had happened. It is dangerous when we suffer a lot, not to arrive at consensus not to keep suffering but to survive; otherwise people will tread all over us until we feel completely massacred and dead after people have discovered our weaknesses. We may end up being ridiculed or people may start playing with our feelings. It is important to redirect our energies towards the horizon of humanity. Please, do not be sad; rather see the circumstance as a passing one in order to reach out to the one who truly appreciates us. Only you can make me happy...

10

Song of Freedom

"Free at last, Free at last, Thank God almighty we are free at last." (1963)

Martin Luther King Jr., *I Have a Dream: Writings and Speeches That Changed the World* (2003)

The Eagle.
©Barbosa Archives 2015

Though not intended to be linear or chronological, the ending of this narrative plot turns out to be circular by sheer coincidence. "Free at last" echoes a singular meaning for most African Americans who were fortunate witnesses of the Martin Luther King Jr.'s "I Have a Dream" (1963) speech when it was delivered in Washington D.C. five decades ago. It was about hope. Yet, the double entendre implicit in that speech and the ripples it sent through the American system, left no doubt in anyone's mind about its prophetic impact. In the end, what was a rallying call to the Nation through the "March on Washington," was also a decision to take a bold stand against racial discrimination. In addition, it was an invitation to racial justice that turned historic in the sense that no one could have predicted that the speech signaled that Mr. King's days were numbered due to racial hatred and violence. The freedom articulated in "Free at last" became not just freedom from racism that was dispossessing many African Americans, as in the post-slavery context, but also signaled the civil rights leader and the possibility of losing his life for his social activism. Notwithstanding, the impact of that freedom resonated around the world. For that Herculean sacrifice, we are all very grateful for a life that was unnecessarily truncated but also monumentalized in the process. I borrow from the strength of this opening epilogue and the moral power entrenched in the entire speech to situate the legacy of Lúcia; not because there is a comparative level of sacrifice per se, but because of the depth of personal sacrifice that I believe Lúcia's life represents for me. It is more homage than a parallel. This is more of an invocation than a conflation. It is more of a symbolic frame of consciousness than an attempt to insinuate the slightest similarity. Lúcia gave up the ghost in the process of helping others. She was in a sense a selfless activist in the socio-philosophical order of things. It is a season of freedom for her because she no longer has to deal with the vicissitudes of this life. This segment returns to the recuperation of her memories as I have done in the entire narrative, synthesizing our shared but fleeting romantic moments over many decades of presence, absence, and cosmic communication, as well as the ultimate agonizing moment when she suddenly succumbed to a terminal disease in a rather dramatic way.

Given the unintended emotional closure, the narrative will be mixed and varied as it goes back and forth between reality and fantasy, perhaps in order to mediate the pain of loss. It is a season of freedom, indeed, but also of agony about the irreparable disappearance of a soul that should still be in our midst.. All that I have left are intense memories. I feel her entire enduring spirit weighing on me. At times, the memories even overpower me. I need energy to be able to process this irreplaceable loss. I console myself in Mother Nature mostly, and in what Lúcia talked about in her cosmic writings that are now lost but regained from their tangible essence to the elusive process of begging for recuperation through the power of reconstructing past memories and recreating newly invented memories and invocations. I hear the voice of Lúcia confirming to me that all is well with her; that this closure must be celebrated, rather than mourned. It must not ever be perceived as a sad farewell. I reach out for the memories I hold most vividly in her most recent words: "Congratulations, You are winning. You are shining. You are a bright light within the Divine Plan. You are winning and will win and overcome everything and everyone. You are very special, a godsend. I believe in you. You will achieve more than you can even imagine!" This was the last communication I remember from Lúcia. It felt just like yesterday. And now comes her voice, once again, as a form of puzzling closure for this esoteric narrative.

I, Lúcia, come in my Yoruba name, Moremi. I now live among the Orisas. I am Moremi. Through sacrifice, giving myself to humanity, I am Mother Land, I am Cosmic Mother, I am Immortality. I know you have been concerned about me. I am doing just fine in the spiritual realm. We should celebrate the times we had to express our transcendental humanity. My destiny is not of this world. I am the past, the present and the future; not divine but an agent of goodness in the troubling world of which you are still part. There were so many memories we did not get to share or complete. Our communication was suddenly interrupted by the fragilities of the flesh. I want to help fill some of the missing links for you, to the best of my ability. I start by greeting you in Yoruba: "*Ilera, alafia, ife, ati imole pupo ni fun e!*" [May health, peace, love and much light be yours!]. Ah, you did not know I learned to speak Yoruba, right? I did everything to surprise you. I am still a surprise to you, right? I am now teasing you as we are used to teasing each other. You help me fulfill all my dreams and those of my children I left behind. They tell me you are in their lives. All grown and with children. But Fayola seems to have been more resistant to family life. What can we possibly do? I have always known that. She likes her freedom from her tender age. She is very adventurous. She is not the settling down type. She enjoys her esoteric adventures. It is better not to push her too much. She is not in a hurry to settle down to a family life. I communicate with her spiritually. I strengthen her in my own way. The fact is that she has strengthened herself. Aisha has taken after me a lot. She is more down to earth than naively ambitious. Sandro has actually turned his life around in terms of perseverance and focus. He is with a better group of influences now. He has also lost a lot of weight! Incredible! I am pleased to see they are all doing well. I am happy to see my grandchildren. You must ask Sandro to take you to my graveside when next you visit São Paulo. There are some rituals I want you to perform there in the presence of my children. I want my children to learn how ancestrality works in Yoruba culture so they can return to do the same thing when they are older. They are still mourning my sudden celestial departure, you know. I want you to teach them about the Yoruba cycle of life. I will also teach you to communicate with them when you are on site. You will feel my energies; and you can tell them my wishes. Clétus, you are the most handsome man I have ever met in all my life. You are a divine error to have been born in this era of chaos. Only you can make me happy...

Do you remember the occasions you followed me to my evening school after work from USP? We held hands and your eyes were staring deeply into mine. Were those not special moments, my beloved Clétus? Today, I am now facing the end of the week. I just returned not long ago from the streets. I worked as an invigilator for FUVEST, the entity in charge of *vestibular*, the entrance examination into USP. Since Friday, my life has been somewhat stressed out. I attended Sandro's preschool graduation on Friday. I also had two final exams on the same day and was still able to go to my brother's book launch. Can you imagine so many events crammed into one single day in addition to regular work? And as I was returning home, I got a flat tire. Damn! One must be very strong, believe me! When I got home (as usual) some of your letters were waiting for me, and I could observe the solidification of telepathic and cosmic transmission between us when you stated: "Lúcia, I don't know if you perceive something, but there is something very mysterious about us that may be peculiar to our personality. At times, before you ask about something, I have addressed it, or you have raised it in another discussion. Very interesting and stimulating." That is exactly what I was hoping for at the end of our cosmic communication. That we somehow feel close to each other despite the distance. Where on earth does this kind of telepathy occur as frequently as it happens between us? How many people on earth have this unique privilege of having access to fascinating mysteries and telepathies? Only a few people or perhaps just us, I wonder. This uniqueness in understanding each other, caring for each other, drawing each other closer (among other reasons I am yet to decipher), may be one of the reasons the Divine Force energized our encounter in the first place. Since I am tired now, I am debating how much I can transmit to you in this fragile frame of mind. Well, my basic message to you continues to be that you should be aware that nothing is achieved in this world without some struggle. Nothing.

For example, I am so excited to let you know that I passed into my third year of college studying Tourism Management. To make it this far, only my family really knows just what the journey has taken out of me. Many times, I made it without a car and sometimes took Sandro with me to classes that did not end until 11pm! At times, I fell asleep on the highway and other times, he fell asleep with me, which was dangerous. Someone needed to be awake. In any case, he has become part of my life's rhythm. I have had to stay up into the wee hours of the morning, trying to help him complete his homework and mine since we always got home so late. Even when I had a steady car and there was a party I had to attend, he was always with me. It was tough. It was rough. What do you have to tell me about all of this challenge? You think it is easy? But we took everything in good spirits, as a necessary struggle, a challenge, a defined objective… and at times upon getting home around midnight, the struggle continued. I had to get his clothes ready for the following day, as well as get myself ready for the next day. Today, we can say it paid off and we are reaping the benefits of those sacrifices.

I believe that is the attitude it takes darling. When we want something badly enough, we will find all the necessary determination and willpower to make it happen. What does this determination entail? It means stubbornness in the positive sense. Being persistent, following through, and always being ahead of the game so as not to lag behind. That is the dogged spirit of success. There were days in which I cried. I really cried out of pain and anguish. I was so tired and exhausted. But there is a huge difference in your case. I am facing difficulties where I was born and my whole family is supportive. It does make a difference. I assure you that soon enough, you will be with the one who will make you feel well and happy. It is a matter of time. Once you are able to overcome the passing challenges you are facing now, you will become a hero, and you are already overcoming a huge part of the battles ahead. You have overcome the inner battle: the battle of deprivation of affection, love, and culture. Then you are struggling to overcome the daily challenges of petty rivalry and jealousies at work and in school. Oh by the way, I dreamed that someone sent me a message from you saying that you asked me to forget about coming to see you in the USA. What a nightmare! Is this fantasy or reality? I miss you very much. Only you can make me happy…

Yesterday, I dispatched a mail to you that must have been about t10 pages. I am not sure what I was thinking and all that I wanted to communicate to you. After you read them, I would like to get your feedback. My sweet and darling Clétus, I just want you to know that I miss you a lot and it is a good thing to be able to say it feels good to love and embrace each other with words of affection and compassion. Even longing is not as bad a feeling to have and to know that one is feeling intense emotions about another special person. In today's newspapers, everyone is complaining about the rise in gasoline cost. It has already risen twice and will rise for the third time, but Brazilians do not do anything. Everyone is afraid. Afraid of being jailed, tortured, or killed. As a result, most people accept the status-quo as the norm. Personally, I don't want to die for anything except for love; in fact, I do not want to die; I just want to love. I send you energy of love, affection, peace, and vitality. I love you like I have never loved anyone before. I wish you would comment on my efforts to speak with you in your Nigerian or

Yoruba language. Why are you not responding to my efforts? It is impossible not to reach out to you every day. It is a good feeling. I am glad you feel the same way. You are such a unique being. You will always succeed. I know you will!

On many occasions, perhaps for my own selfish reasons, I wish I could persuade you to return to Brazil. Yet, seeing things from a more realistic and non-sentimental perspective, I would urge you to keep trying to the best of your abilities until you reach the limits of your energy, survival instincts, and struggle to attain your objective. If the outcomes remain negative and you feel your defined objectives are weakened or no longer attainable, and nothing is making sense any more, then I urge you not to lose your mind or health over such a material goal. On the other hand, imagine what it would add to your professional profile. I am sure it will open other distinguished doors for you once you complete your studies in the USA. It may be better to complete the program now in misery than to do it in the future in happiness. I believe nothing is per chance and I believe there may be something for you to learn from this experience once you persevere and complete it at all cost. We have a saying in Brazil that no difficult time lasts forever. It feels like the Americans have captured you as they did Kunta Kinte in *Roots*[1], where they gave him a different name after being forcibly removed from Africa, and for refusing a foreign name, he was beaten into submission. I think your situation is much better than that of Kunta Kinte. You have a freedom of will to stay or to leave. I know this is not funny to you.

Feel free to choose. Ask yourself if you are feeling so uptight due to pride, status, the system, the set objectives, or the dream to be transformed into a famous person. There is something to be proud of in the future; to say that you earned your doctorate

---

1   See Alex Haley, *Roots: The Saga of an American Family* (New York: Doubleday, 1976); see also the film version, *Roots* [30th anniversary edition] (New York: Warner Brothers, 2011).

in the USA or simply that you fulfilled your dreams in spite of the odds. As long as you are determined to pay the price for your objectives, everything is possible. Personally, I have had many disappointments, anxieties, and crises just like you and I am also very sensitive. How did I manage to overcome the odds? I have always wanted to go to CAMPINAS, another university that is one hour away from USP. But something kept me thinking. Anything done impulsively is never well done. So one needs to let the moment of revolt and pain pass first, and then with sustained enthusiasm, reflect to make a wiser decision. I may receive an invitation now to be the Executive Assistant to the Vice Chancellor of USP. Of course, I would be excited. I will even throw a party. But before accepting the position I have to weigh the pros and cons and see if this is what I really want; is it the status or my own inner peace? Our goal is what shows us the path to take. I know with the incentives and the positive encouragement I am giving you, I may be the one running the risk of not ever seeing you again once you achieve your dreams, but I leave everything in the hands of God. I think it is better to respect people and their objectives. May the will of God be done in our lives. Only you can make me happy...

    My own battle on this side of the Atlantic is parallel to your experience. I have now passed to the third year of college in Tourism Management and my plan is to pursue a Master's in Business Marketing and a doctorate in Marketing Management if conditions permit. Even after feeling a sense of accomplishment, I feel as if it was not enough to have won my battles. I cannot make sense of my tiredness and why I am so weak even after winning the war. I am also thinking of moving to another Unit within USP. I think I have completed my mission here at the Institute of Advanced Studies. At this juncture, I am not likely to have any form of promotion or professional advancement. I also got an offer to join the Museum of Contemporary Art, but my condition was to wait until they complete building their headquarters here on USP campus instead of at the Ibirapuera Park where they are currently located. I love the USP campus and from the research I have done, it is the best in South America; thus I want to remain here if at all possible. I find everything I want here at this University: the green environment, hospital, metropolitan landscapes, restaurants, pharmacy, laboratories, and a little bit of chaos and noise that a metropolis needs. I am enjoying the positive feedback you are giving me about making progress with your work and assignments. Despite the daily and institutional challenges, you are proving that you are determined to succeed. I could not believe my eyes when I read your mail addressing me as "my darling wife." I was overjoyed. You added: "Let me seize this opportunity to say that I am full of emotions but I try not to cry. How long are we going to continue this cosmic communication? Where and when are we going to get married?" I accept your proposal and say yes, I want to marry you as long as this is what you want. Marriage is beautiful, but also very mystical.

Marital life requires a lot of creativity, dedication, love and respect. I will even accept to marry you today as long as both of us discuss our expectations from the relationship, our individual and collective objectives, as well as a sense of complementarity between us. We have been on this journey for a long time. Our mystical, transcendental, cosmic, and intellectual conversation assures me that you are the perfect man for me. You will surely understand me. We have so many things in common. You also give me the impression that I will be able to understand you since both of us are so acutely sensitive. Pretenders are many but I finally found the right person: You! Notwithstanding the divine aura between us, I still feel a little insecure though. I wonder if you are proposing to me just out of being lonely in the USA? I would like to get married in Brazil. I also feel an internal peace about everything. There is nothing to worry about. God is with us. Our Christmas and festivities for the New Year went well with the whole family embracing each other. Strangely, even my dad asked of you: "When is Clétus coming back?" He completely gave me the shock of my life. I did not realize the whole family was spying on our relationship. Though you are not telling much about your family in Nigeria, I thought I should ask you anyway. How are they doing? Are they in touch with you? I hope it is fine with you that I ask about your family. I appreciate the fact that there is not even the slightest sign of selfishness between us. Even before you traveled, you consulted with me and we both decided that it was best that you went first and we will see what else to do afterwards.

Every day I contemplate you as the divine error made exclusively for my happiness. Today, I think I will go out with a neighbor to a bar where there will be some live music. My sister and Sandro sent some brief notes to you trying to convince you to return to Brazil. They all miss you. I am getting ready mentally to visit you in July. I am already imagining smelling your body and passing my hands all over you. My birthday is on the 3rd of July and that of my sister's is on the 4th of July. I will buy my ticket a month before departure. It is now about 10pm. I am getting ready to go out with my neighbors. I am in front of the mirror; all dressed up. I can see you asking me questions and commenting on my looks. I am listening to blues and thinking of you. Please do not hurt me, just make me happy always. We came back from the bar at 4am and I slept until 1pm the following day. It is now my turn to cry on your shoulder. Though I was around many people at the bar, I felt so lonely because you were not there with me. That is why I ask many questions and at times, you do not respond. Are my anxieties normal or crazy? Am I too demanding in my series of questions? Feel free to respond in your own way. Do not feel pressured to answer what you don't feel like answering. My sweet love, I just miss you so much.

Dear Lúcia, Now that you have filled the gaps your own way as you pleaded with me to do, it is my turn to provide the missing links after life stopped our cosmic communication for good or for ill. It is quite a huge challenge to package a 20-year gap into a short story. You ended up not visiting me in the USA. I did complete my degree but later decided to settle down in the country to grow professionally. The next time we met was in 1993 when I made the first attempt to bring my Brazilian son to the USA. You had just given birth to Fayola. I was pleased to witness that experience. The other time we met was at the Guarrulhos Airport in São Paulo in 1998. Since then, my visits became more frequent in the 1990s when I was doing research for a book on Afro-Brazilian literature. For about five years, I visited you in São Paulo every year before going to other parts of Brazil, especially Bahia. By the time I was professionally stable to even reward you with the English as a second language summer program, you were called into the beyond. Much of the details were kept from me until it was too late. I only got the news that you were hospitalized and I wanted to speak with you. This was very painful for me. All you could tell me then was that you had contracted a gangrene in one of your feet. It was cancerous and terminal. The emotions were high. We believed God would grant us a miracle. I just could not even imagine death as a possibility until I got the scary call that you were gone. How could you have left me just like that? The year was 2002. Exactly 20 years since we met. What does it all mean? How do I cope with this unexpected bereavement?

It is amazing how dreams do or do not always come true. Yet, for a soul such as Lúcia, the force of the dreams fulfilled through just being human lingers on. We may not have shared longer years together but the rare quality moments we shared are constant reminders of the will of two beings who were profoundly in love. I am still not in full grasp of the notion of your departure. Why did it have to be so soon? You left no clues that you were in such a haste to leave this world of chaos and confusion. My soul is troubled, but I am also at peace because that is the way you would have wanted it. As this narrative winds to a close, I am compelled to briefly reflect on issues of life and death. If there is something called the afterlife, I would like to see you there. Your gentle soul, your acts of love, your affection, your compassion, and your generosity are all the elements that make this departure even the more traumatic and unbearable. I am puzzled that this life is so fragile. The dreams of being together as one, getting married and having children, and making the world a better place are suddenly gone. I beg of you, forget not the ones you left behind. When I see the beautiful ones you left behind, Sandro, Fayola, and Aisha; I see you. They are all doing well. They turned out remarkably well. You would be proud of them and of yourself. It is something of an irony that whenever I encounter them on social media, they reach out to me, begging me to visit São Paulo, so that we can all tell nostalgic tales, and ultimately say we are not moved. Life has not been fair at all. Fair or not, you left a dose of your humanity within everyone you cared for in life. You are very special. You are truly lovely. You are impeccably beautiful. There is no other just like you. You are greatly missed. While your list of generosities is such that they cannot be repaid, I render this narrative into a song of praise for your gentle soul and peaceful personality. I have called this narrative *Cosmic Whispers* in order to register those special years we spent whispering love and humanity into each other's ears, whether close to each other or far away. I wonder what you would have called it? Perhaps *Cosmic Gatherings*. This is a robust harvest indeed. I assure you that it has become history as you have always wanted it. Remind me once again, "What we write today

Cosmic Whispers

will become history tomorrow"? Yes, today, we begin a virgin page of history in a season of gatherings. Farewell, Lúcia.

Vera Barbosa
©Barbosa Archives 2000

Two generations of Barbosa Family
©Barbosa Archives 2018

Glossary

Afoxé: A carnival group influenced by Africa-derived religion of Candomblé

Alcione Nazaré: One of the most successful female sambistas in Brazil of the late 1970s

August Flower: A poem written for Lúcia in 1982

Axé Music: A musical style of the 1980s mixing samba with reggae, salsa, and Ijexá

Bandejão: Student cafeteria at the University of São Paulo

Beatles: British Rock band that impacted US popular music scene in the 1960s

Beth Carvalho: A Brazilian singer associated with the Mangueira school of samba in Rio

Bhakti: Devotion

Buffalo woman: An embodiment of generosity and hospitality in the Sundiata epic of Mali

Caetano Veloso:	A legendary Brazilian singer and political activist of the Tropicalist group
Carmen Miranda:	The first Brazilian performer and singer to attain international stardom
Camisa Verde:	A school of samba in São Paulo
Candomblé:	Africa-derived Afro-Brazilian religion
Centro Olímpico:	Campus accommodation for international students in Brasília
Circular Bus:	A type of 'subway on wheels' in São Paulo of the 1980s
Clarice Lispector:	A 20th century Brazilian female writer
Clint Eastwood:	An American actor who is well-known for his roles in Western TV shows
CNPq:	A Brazilian funding agency for professors and students
Djavan:	Brazilian musician who fuses Brazilian rhythms with global musical styles
Elza Soares:	A legendary Brazilian singer who interprets classic bossas and sambas
Exu/Eşu	Yoruba deity of the crossroads
Favela:	Brazilian urban slum, often dangerous, where the poorest population lives
Gilberto Gil:	Brazilian singer, songwriter, activist, and Tropicalist movement member
Ilê Aiyê:	Pioneer Afro-carnival group in Salvador-Bahia that was created in 1974
Ivan Lins:	Brazilian popular musician and jazz player for over thirty years

Karma:	Belief that the energy of a person's actions returns to them in the next life
Jnana:	Divine reality
Leci Brandão:	Brazilian singer and composer of Brazilian popular music and pagode
Maria Bethânia:	A legendary Brazilian popular musician especially bossa nova and samba
Mary Tyler Moore:	American actress, known for her roles in the TV sitcom, Mary Tyler Show
Martinho da Vila:	An esteemed Brazilian singer and composer of Brazilian popular music
Merv Griffin:	A singer, movie actor, media mogul, and host of The Merv Griffin Show
Milton Nascimento:	Brazilian singer-songwriter and foremost icon of Brazilian popular music
Minhocão:	A millipede-styled architecture at the University of Brasília
Moremi:	Yoruba woman who sacrificed her only child to save Ile Ife from invaders
Muzenza:	An Afro-carnival group, founded in 1981, refined the samba-reggae style8
Neguinho do Samba:	A percussionist and founder of samba-reggae rhythm in Bahian carnival
Olodum:	An Afro-carnival group, founded in 1979, that promotes samba-reggae
Oprah Winfrey:	An American media executive best known for her 'Oprah Winfrey Show'
Oxum/Oṣun:	Yoruba deity of beauty, fertility, and sweet waters

Pierre Verger:	A Franco-Brazilian photographer and anthropologist
Pixinguinha:	One of the greatest composers of Brazilian pop music especially the *choro*
Quilombhoje:	A collective of Afro-Brazilian writers based in São Paulo
Raja:	Great king
Real:	Brazilian currency
Rodney King:	A central figure in the Los Angeles riot of 1992
Sanatana dharma:	Eternal way
Sandra de Sá:	Popular Brazilian singer and songwriter from Rio de Janeiro
SAP:	Structural Adjustment Program
Umbigada:	Belly dance move in various Afro-Brazilian dances
Vai-Vai:	A school of samba in São Paulo
Vila Isabel:	One of Rio de Janeiro's famous schools of samba
Yoga:	Hindu philosophy that stresses physical and mental discipline for the attainment of liberation from the material world and union of self with the Supreme Being
Zeca Pagodinho:	A Brazilian singer and composer noted for samba and pagode